The Girl Code Manual

Written by:
Ashley Porter, Dae'l Pasco, Jasmine Joseph, Monique Perkins, Teairra Barnes, Brittney Hoover, Dacia Carter, and Tiffany Lindsey

Copyright

The Girl Code Manual © 2021 by Ashley Porter

Printed in the United States of America

ISBN: 978-0-578-76330-9

All rights reserved. No part of this book may be reproduced in any form or by any electronic, mechanical or photocopying or stored in a retrieval system without the written permission of the publisher except by a reviewer who may quote brief passages to be included in a review.

Scripture quotations marked (AMP) are taken from the Amplified Bible, Copyright © 1954, 1958, 1962, 1964, 1965, 1987 by The Lockman Foundation. Used by permission.

Scripture quotations are from the ESV® Bible (The Holy Bible, English Standard Version®), copyright © 2001 by Crossway, a publishing ministry of Good News Publishers. Used by permission. All rights reserved.

Scripture quotations marked MSG are taken from *THE MESSAGE*, copyright © 1993, 2002, 2018 by Eugene H. Peterson. Used by permission of NavPress. All rights reserved. Represented by Tyndale House Publishers, a Division of Tyndale House Ministries.

Scriptures marked KJV are taken from the KING JAMES VERSION (KJV): KING JAMES VERSION, public domain.

Edited by Armor of Hope Writing & Publishing Services

Table of Contents

Prayer 5

A Little Background 7

Introduction 9

Have You Considered my Faithful Servant? 11

Identity Decoded By: Ashley Speaks 21

Mindset Shift By: Jasmine Joseph 29

Receiving God's Love By: Teairra Barnes 43

Purpose Moves: Obedience By: Tiffany Lindsey 57

Scarred for Purpose By: MoNique Perkins 67

Her Beauty Isn't Your Beast By Dae'l Pasco 75

I Promise... -Love always, God, The Promise Keeper 91

Meet the Authors 99

Prayer

Father God, in the name of Jesus, thank you for our sister, your daughter, who is embarking on this journey. May she not only be encouraged and empowered as she reads this book, but may she have an encounter with you that will shift the trajectory of her life. May you open her mind and prepare her for transformation. We come against fear, confusion, depression, trauma, abandonment, lack, low level thinking, generational curses, bondage, brokenness and whatever has been hindering her progress and process to thriving in her purpose. We partner our faith together and declare the chains to be destroyed now in Jesus' mighty name. Lord, we declare and decree that you will speak to her heart throughout the pages of this book. May your will be done in and through your daughter.

Amen

A Little Background

Girl Code was birthed from a message I ministered in February 2020. I actually prepared an entirely different message, but two nights before leaving for Florida, God flipped the script- as usual. The night I was assigned to minister at the "Her Whole Heart" conference in Tampa, Florida, hosted by Dae'l Pasco (you'll read from her in a few), I wrote the prayer pictured below. I was desperate for a fresh encounter with God. I desperately wanted to be used by Him and not just preach a "good word". I decided to include this prayer to share my heart and to show the seed that was sown before all of this took root and began to grow. The "Girl Code" message was truly an on-time word and once released and received nothing has been the same. This book was merely an idea that night and here we are! Be encouraged that your obedience is connected to more than you may ever know. I gathered a few amazing women of God to share what they deem as imperative "codes". We are beyond honored that you are reading this manifested miracle.

It's time to unlock your potential & thrive in your purpose.

-Ashley A. Porter

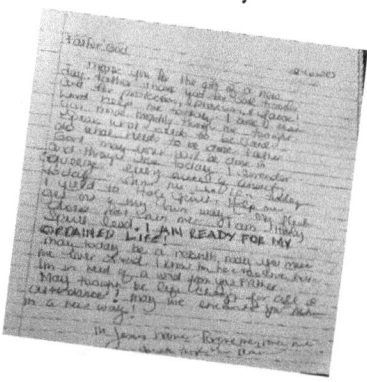

Introduction

The purpose of this book is to equip, encourage, establish, and affirm you. It was imperative for me to gather seven amazing women of God to join me in writing this manual because it's time to collaborate and stop competing. I knew this book was not something Ashley needed to produce but something that would call my sisters out of comfortability, fear, doubt, procrastination, double mindedness, etc. This book is bigger than the vision I saw sitting in Dae'l's Honda in Tampa, Fl in February 2020. This book is bigger than each of us. This book is an answer to a problem. It's a solution for your suffering. It's a blueprint to lead you from brokenness to wholeness. This book was created for purpose and you are reading this at an appointed time. Pray, take notes within the pages provided, answer the questions submitted, and expect a shift.

Have You Considered my Faithful Servant?

By: Brittney B. Hoover

There's Job

One of the most thought-provoking and baffling Bible stories is that of Job. Blameless. Faithful. Devoted. Yet, trouble still found its way into his household, by way of God. Yes, you read that correctly. Even if you have not fully read his story, it is likely you have heard of it. The conversation went something like this: "Now there was a day when the sons of God came to present themselves before the Lord, and Satan came also among them. And the Lord said unto Satan, 'Whence comest thou?' Then, Satan answered the Lord, and said, 'From going to and fro in the earth, and from walking up and down in it.' And the Lord said unto Satan, 'Hast thou considered my servant Job, that there is none like him in the earth, a perfect and an upright man, one that feareth God, and escheweth evil?'" (Job 1:6-8, KJV).

Wow! When read in the natural, it is easy for one to think to themselves, "Why would God present his own servant to the enemy?" The trouble that is on its way into Job's life catches him by surprise, yet it does not catch God by surprise because he approves it. Yes, he loves Job, and Job loves him, but he allows the enemy to test Job's faith. Chapters and chapters of suffering makes believers feel a level of pity and empathy for Job. One messenger does not leave before another reports to Job with notice of loss, after loss, after loss. Mind-blown, every believer reads to the end, hoping and believing for victory on Job's behalf.

Then There's You It is rather convenient for us to see our battles as physical. As women, we often encounter issues and conflicts that seemingly get the best of us: the man on the highway with the road rage, the lady in the grocery store who is disgruntled that we are taking so long to load our groceries on the belt, our friends who disagree with our life decisions, and so much more. If we are not prayerful, careful, and mindful of the spirituality in all of these types of situations, we are in for a rude awakening.

Opposition will come. Heartache and headache will come. How we respond to these things will determine how we overcome them. Truthfully, we are in a spiritual war daily. Whether we desire to be or not, every time we put our feet on the floor, our enemy is waging a war against the God who is in us. His attacks are personal, as he hates who abides in us. So, let's talk about it. Let's expose the enemy for who he is and become fully aware of what his intent is, how he strategizes and why. When we know the enemy and his tactics, we are more prepared to win in the spiritual realm. We do not have to succumb to the attacks of the enemy. He is subtle, sneaky, and predictable. It is time for women to rise up and walk in total victory.

The Word

As believers, we have one weapon that is proven to work-The Word. Despite who or what we encounter during this life, we must rest assured that the black letters on white pages that we tote to the prayer room and to the sanctuary pack a powerful punch. When the words on these pages become written on our hearts and engrafted in our spirits, we find a cure for every disease. Your ailment may not be mine, and mine may not be yours; however, the word of God is authentic and true.

So, what does the word of God say about spiritual warfare? Ephesians 6: 10-18 declares, "Finally, my brethren, be strong in the Lord, and in the power of his might. Put on the whole armour of God, that ye may be able to stand against the wiles of the devil.

For we wrestle not against flesh and blood, but against principalities, against powers, against the rulers of the darkness of this world, against spiritual wickedness in highplaces. Wherefore take unto you the whole armour of God, that ye may be able to withstand in the evil day, and having done all, to stand. Stand therefore, having your loins girt about with truth, and having on the breastplate of righteousness; And your feet shod with the preparation of the gospel of peace; Above all, taking the shield of faith, wherewith ye shall be able to quench all the fiery darts of the wicked. And take the helmet of salvation, and the sword of the Spirit, which is the word of God: Praying always with all prayer and supplication in the Spirit and watching thereunto with all perseverance and supplication for all saints." Carefully outlined in this passage is the reality that believers will face challenges. These challenges are never with people but spirits and the armor needed to overcome said challenges. Sisters, all we need is within us.

All we need to fight our battles in the spiritual realm dwells inside of us. We need a relationship with God. We need to suit up in his armor, and we need to believe that God calls us to rest, cast our cares on him, and suit up in his armor, not our own. The word of God is filled with regular people with a measure of faith, who were often faced with indescribable tasks and challenges that may have seemed grandiose but were overcome through the strength of God.

The War

Ladies, we can wear our make-up, shop 'til we drop, post the cutest pictures and videos onto social media, but are we prepared for the war that is brewing every time we set our feet on the floor? Again, there is indeed a spiritual war brewing whether we like it to or not. I have discovered this war often occurs right between our two ears. All too often, we give in to the spiritual war waging in our minds-the war between what the Lord has promised and what we see that may even align to the lies the enemy is whispering to us. Can we just be transparent and admit that we find ourselves in the midst of spiritual mayhem because what we see and what God said does not match up, but sometimes what we see matches up with what the enemy is whispering? Where does that leave us? It leaves us in position to believe the King of all Kings and take him at his word or believe the lies the master of falsehood is implanting in our spirits. Sister, I have compiled a list of lies the enemy has whispered to me over the years.

Identify the ones you can relate to as you read:

I am not worthy of God's love.
I don't do enough; I am not enough.
My gifts are not "all that."
I can't.
I am not a leader.
I am not a business-minded woman.
I'll do "it" later. There's no urgency to do "it" now.
I don't want _____ (Insert anything you claim to not want but you actually do
want.)

We could all add several bullet points to this list, but I am sure we can all relate to one or more of these listed, and the truth is if it finds itself on this list, it is rooted in a lie and does not come from our heavenly Father.

The Win

That brings us to the win. We know there is an enemy with targets on our minds and our relationship with the Father. We know the biggest war to ever occur is in our mind. Having been equipped to know about the war, we must feel just as equipped for the win!

Sisters, the first reality we must all embrace is the truth that the victory was won over 2000 years ago. Jesus Christ set the stage for us all to walk in victory. If we believe in Jesus, his life, burial and resurrection, we must believe we have access to all that is his. We are a royal priesthood, and we are recipients of every promise ever made in the word of God. Out of his mouth and into our hearts is the truth, nothing less.

The second reality is that we do not wage war as the world does. We march into victory in the heavenly realm, not in a physical one. Our fight is fixed. We have the spiritual weapons needed to shut the enemy down! You are more than a conqueror, and you have power that you haven't even used, power you are completely unaware of but still possess. Use that power. Luke 10:19 (KJV) declares, "Behold, I give unto you power to tread on serpents and scorpions, and over all the power of the enemy: and nothing shall by any means hurt you." This is a non-negotiable truth. Believers pack power!

Lastly, reflect on the movie previews you see in the movie theater. They show the highlights; they show just enough to get viewers intrigued. If they showed every detail, there would be no reason to come back to watch the entire movie. If they showed the most boring or saddest scenes, you would be prepared to skip over them, close your eyes, or whatever it took to not view the most agitating and predictable scenes. Ladies, this defines the life of a believer. We have the promise. We know what God has said to us, whispered to us in the valley, or given to us in a vision. We have the end, but we get discouraged along the way. We get sidetracked by the waging wars in our minds, in our households, in our communities. Truthfully, if we knew every detail leading to the promises of God, we would take another route. Much like Jonah, we would give God a resounding no! That is why we must hold on to the victory, trusting the God of details far more than the details themselves. Details waver, God does not.

God is reminding us in these pages to keep our eyes fixed on His promises, even when our circumstances say differently, even when the enemy slithers in and whispers lie after lie. Our fight is never carnal; it is always spiritual, and we must take hold of that truth. Let us put on the whole armor of God and combat every lie of the enemy with the word of God.

After This

After Job lost it all, there was an "after this" experience. Job lived his best life after having seemingly lost it all. Despite what Job lost, he did not lose it all. He did not lose his hunger for God. He did not lose the victory. In the midst of spiritual warfare, with a mouth full of questions and a heart filled with hurt, Job did not abandon his relationship with God. "After this lived Job a hundred and forty years, and saw his sons, and his sons' sons, even four generations" (Job 42:16, KJV).

Queens, there is a war waging, but be encouraged that this war has already been won. We are fighting a fixed fight, and as believers, we have the necessary tools to walk in victory. Just as Job, there will be an "after this" for us all. The reality is that for every lie, the living and breathing word has provided truth. This truth we must continuously remind ourselves of in order to operate in victory as opposed to defeat.

We must fight in the strength of God, not our own. The word declares us winners. It is so, and it shall not be otherwise.

Questions to Consider:
1. How do you generally deal with hardship? How will that improve today?
2. What lie can you replace with truth? Jot down every lie the enemy tells you frequently and find a scripture that dismantles that lie.
3. In what ways do you relate to the story of Job?
4. What does the word say about hardships and how we are to overcome?
5. Who or what do you often deem responsible for hardships and losses in your life? Does seeing things spiritually as opposed to naturally change that for you?
6. Job had an "after this" experience. For what part of your life do you decree and declare an "after this?"
7. We do not wage war as mere humans do. We put on the whole armor of God. What does this look like in your daily life?

_____
_____
_____
_____
_____
_____
_____
_____
_____
_____
_____

Identity Decoded

By: Ashley Speaks

Knowing who you are is a layered process. Be very clear in knowing that life is NOT linear. Identity is crucial to lay hold, but identity is also not to be confused with labels. You know, they say you're funny. They say you're loud. They say you're dumb. They say you do too much. They say you're too inquisitive. They say you're fat. They say you're too skinny. They say you're too light or too dark. Whatever the label is, if it's not found in the word of God, sis, you do not have to put it on.

We live in a society where we expect things immediately. We expect a husband or wife that is "no bake." You know how they have no bake lasagna noodles. That's exactly it. We expect entry level positions making six figures. We want end products without enduring and growing through the process. At the age of twenty-three, I found myself shifting. I no longer desired to live and do things routinely. I remember asking myself, "Is this it? Is this all my life will be?" It was as if I woke up, as if I snapped out of a daze. I recount this encounter in my first book "Basic Training: How to Prepare for your Spiritual Quest" but It's necessary to share it in this necessary "Code" about identity.

One day, I was walking up the stairs to my apartment and I felt a ceiling above me. I couldn't step up or back down. I was stuck! I heard an audible voice, "This is as far as you will go if you continue to do things your way." Being stagnant was a struggle, not because I didn't believe I deserved better out of life, but because I knew shifting would cost me things. I didn't know how to attain a better life, the best life. I then heard, "By operating at a lower level you are simply helping the devil." I immediately said, "Nah, that's not me! I don't want to help the devil." I went inside and prayed. I asked God to wreck me. I asked him to wreck my friendships, my relationship, my dreams, ideas, thoughts; wreck everything that I did myself. If anything in my life was from my own doing, I didn't want any parts of it. I truly got extremely desperate to live the life God created me to live. Living a life that I created was purposeless. Nothing has been the same since that night. I want to dispel the notion that walking in purpose and living a renewed life in Christ immediately changes *everything*. Contrary to popular belief, there is definitely a process to purpose. The one thing that does immediately change is your eternity. Your thoughts, your actions; your life literally enters a process, a process that is like what happens to precious metals such as silver and gold. Fire refining is how these metals are refined and purified. According to Wikipedia, "In metallurgy, refining consists of purifying an impure metal. It is to be distinguished from other processes such as smelting and calcining. Those two involve a chemical change to the raw material. Whereas in refining, the final material is usually identical chemically to the original one, only it is purer."

In 2017, Holy Spirit told me that fire consumes, but it also refines and purifies. There's a purpose for the fire. There's a purpose for the hurt, the pain, and the trial. There is a purpose for that situation and circumstance that seems unbearable. Gold and silver must be placed directly in the middle of the fire and the silversmith cannot take their eyes off of it while it's in the fire, or it will be ruined. Like a silversmith, our Heavenly Father is always watching over us. He never leaves us nor forsakes us. Contrary to how you feel, the fire you may find yourself in the middle of will not consume you, it's preparing you. However, the fire in your life has come to consume the lies of the enemy, the lack, the poverty, the ill mindset, the misconstrued outlook, low self-esteem, and feelings of inadequacy. Everything contrary to your true identity and purpose in Christ, the fire is sent to consume. The fire in your life has come to refine you. The situation may hurt and is uncomfortable, but it's refining you. Refine means to remove impurities or unwanted elements. The fire has come to remove the impurities that have taken root in you. Purification is the removal of contaminants, the things that are hindering you and keeping you stagnant, and in some cases, immobile. The fear, the doubt, the shame, the guilt- has to go.

Perspective is everything and how we approach situations and daily life are either helping you to reflect Christ or reflect a contaminated replica. Enduring the process builds your character, and your trust in God. The more you endure the more you rely on the Father and not people or things. Thank you for sacrificing time to invest in your soul health.

Your character is what people remember. Character is what qualifies us for opportunities and advancement. Our character lets others know we can be trusted. Our character lets God know if we're prepared. Character is vital to our everyday life. Your persona is not your character; it's an aspect but not the totality of your character. Here is a quick nugget about persona. Your public persona and private persona should not be on opposite ends of the spectrum. What do you mean, Ashley? I mean there's no need to be fake. Be who you are and get to the root of why you are that way. If you're mean, there's an area of your heart that's hardened, and God wants to heal you, but He's the ultimate gentleman. He's waiting for the invitation to enter in. If you're bitter, God wants to remove that bitterness and give you joy. If you're fearful, God wants to give you an infusion of faith to overcome that fear. Hear me, God cannot acknowledge what you refuse to identify. We have to be accountable and responsible.

I believe it's imperative to know who and whose you are because 1 Peter 5:8 tells us, "Be sober- minded; be watchful. Your adversary the devil prowls around like a roaring lion, seeking someone to devour." John 10:10 says, "The thief comes only to steal and kill and destroy. I came that they may have life and have it abundantly." 2 Corinthians 2:11 says, "So that we would not be outwitted by Satan; for we are not ignorant of his designs." Ephesians 6:11 says, "Put on the whole armor of God, that you may be able to stand against the schemes of the devil. All of these scriptures tell us the plan of Satan. They give us insight into his intentions. If you know whose you are, you are less likely to fall for the schemes of Satan. If you know your identity through Christ and actually walk in that identity unapologetically, you won't be tripped up over contrary thoughts, lying labels, and plans sent to derail and distract you. Knowing your identity is a weapon. I've learned that knowing is not enough; it's imperative to believe what you know. Think about it like this. You buy a new bed. It comes with all the parts and instructions so you have all that you need to properly assemble your new bed, but if you don't believe that you're capable of assembling the bed correctly, it will stay in a box, and you'll continue looking at the pretty picture on the box instead of enjoying the bed in its intended purpose.

Tis the season to thrive, sis. There's never been a more perfect moment than today, to commit to doing the inner work. Take the time to invest in your healing and wholeness. Learn to love yourself and see yourself the way God does. You aren't the sum total of your past. A pastor I know used to say, "The rearview mirror is smaller because we're not going that way." It's time to intentionally move forward with hope, faith, and expectation. You are who God says you are. PERIOD.

I'm passionate about identity because I remember battling with concealing who I believed I really was. I literally felt like I was in a tug of war. Maybe then it was an act of spiritual warfare. Think about the butterfly. It willingly enters into a period of darkness with confidence that it will only last for a designated period of time. Sis, to discover who God has truly created you to be, you have to get alone with God. You have to get quiet and remove yourself from the distractions and noise of the world. There are so many things pulling at you for your attention, but when you are intentional about intimacy with God, He begins to speak and move in and through you in new ways. This process of unbecoming and rebirth is a lifelong journey. You will always be learning more about you, but I desire for you to get your roots firm. May the truth of who you are be anchored to the revelation from God's word. May you walk with your head high, knowing you are God's handiwork, fearfully and wonderfully made, forgiven, called, purposed, favored, and the head and not the tail. Know that this journey of life will throw a lot at you, but you must be firm in your roots so when distractions come you won't budge at the appearance of a "good" thing and be able to identify a God thing. You can see who someone believes they are by just looking at their life. Who are they around? What are they doing/producing? What are they reading? What are they speaking? Your life speaks louder than your words.

One of my favorite women in the Bible is the woman at the well (John 4). She was broken. She was hurt. She was overlooked and counted out. She made decisions based on lies, not facts. She did what she could, but one encounter with the King changed her forever. Her encounter with Jesus opened her mind up to the truth that she was made for more. She didn't have to settle in any area of her life. That is my prayer for you. Yes, YOU! I pray as you read this and the other "Codes" in this book that you will have an encounter with the King of Kings and the Lord of Lords, that you will begin to truly believe God's truth about you.

<u>Questions to ponder:</u>
1. What does scripture say about identity?
2. What are your ideal character traits? What is hindering you from possessing those traits?
3. What are two ways you can start shifting your perspective about who you are?
4. What may have been said to shape your perception of yourself negatively? Positively?
5. Who do YOU say you are?
6. _____

Mindset Shift

By: Jasmine Joseph

CODE: Mindset Shift! Girl code is giving yourself room to grow once you know better-- in your friendships, relationships, and view of God! Tune in as we get honest with ourselves to finally live out the liberty given to us through Christ. Get ready for your, "Me too, sis" moments! There is something so powerful about the mind and what we know. What we know shapes our actions, whether into destiny or into a place of bondage. The Bible makes it clear to "be transformed by the renewing of your mind" (Romans 12:2). There is a popular saying going around Al Gore's internet that states, "Let's normalize" and it's followed by unhealthy minds sets that we are dedicated to shift. Not only as a woman, but as a black Christian woman, it triggered areas in me that I know we all can benefit from.

This topic is necessary. If we're honest with ourselves, we will admit that our views on numerous areas in our life are shaped by trauma. Our relationship with God is standoffish because of our parental issues. Our lack of genuine friendships is tainted because a few people that weren't trustworthy scarred you years ago. Our views on marriage are tainted because we never saw a healthy marriage growing up. The list goes on. What if I told you, how you've always thought is not how you have to continue thinking? For someone who is all for helping others, I could not leave my sisters out blind, so buckle up, beautiful, and come along!

Friendships

Let's start with friendships. In my sister Ashley's voice, "Somebody shout GIRL CODE." How many times have you heard women say, "I just don't get along with females," or "I only hang out with men because I don't like females?" It's crazy that society has shaped us to have unhealthy views on sisterhood. Now, not everyone is purposed to be your destiny friend or to walk through life with you. Having acquaintances is normal. The problem occurs when you're so bound by the "bad" apples that you block godly ordained friendships to be birthed. For many of us, these unhealthy mindsets have clung to us for more years than not. These mindsets are all that we know, and some people may be deemed "stuck in their ways," but hear me clear, it is not too late to heal! God created us as relational beings, which means we are not meant to do life alone.

While being a Christian does not become the bonding tool for us to be God ordained covenant friends or even do business together. However, we are all to do life with some people! Unfortunately, a lot of people aren't open to any friendships because of the past hurt from other women! We pray and ask God for friendships, yet we aren't friendly. Now, that's Bible. Use wisdom, discernment and God's leading with all things, but I wonder how many of us are missing out because we are scarred from friendships God never led us to be in! Would you believe me if I told you that me and the visionary of this project, Ashley, just met for the first time seven months ago? When I tell you, God brought us together, to be friends through our friend Dae'l, and now they can't get rid of me—our friendship has shifted my life for the better in such a short time of us all meeting only a short time ago. What if I was hesitant, not friendly or didn't open myself up to be led by God? I would have missed this beautiful opportunity for
sisterhood.

Kingdom women are not mean girls. We don't gossip or intentionally slander each other! Even Jesus had friends. He had people that he walked through life with. Then, he had people who were in his inner circle where he literally showed himself being transfigured, only opening himself up to those closest to him, but still he had friends, nevertheless. There is purpose for every person God puts in your life, no matter the amount of time that season may last for, but you have to open yourselves up. I see so many people who desire real friendships yet won't put themselves out there. I am not saying that you have to have tons of girls as friends, but I do want you to be healed and not be so skeptical. I wonder how many of you are missing out on having what Jonathon was to David—a friend that is closer than a brother. Use wisdom, but I don't want you to miss the beauty of sisterhood because of failed friendships in the past.

Relationships

Shifting your mindset is you coming into agreement with Gods word. Once we are saved and adopted into the kingdom of God, the Bible tells us, "We are new creatures in Christ Jesus" (2 Corinthians 5:17). The problem occurs because a lot of us still operate from a place of bondage. Our identities after salvation are still tied to who we were, and we live from that place. When the Bible tells us to "Be transformed by the renewing of your minds," it is not optional. Renewing our minds is the route to walking in freedom. For too long we have allowed who hurt us to dictate how we love, so let's go ahead and dig into relationships.

I don't know about you, but I have had moments in past relationships that could have really put a stamp on how I think relationships go. Now, this was not my exact past experience, but I know this is for someone—I like to call this the "Baby Boy" syndrome. I'm referring to the movie, which happens to be one of my favorites, and don't quote it around me because I'm going to finish every line. If you are not familiar with the movie, it is about a young man who is a "mama's boy." Jody, the main character, has two different baby mamas and creeps around endlessly on his main girl, aka, first baby mama, but "he lies to her because he loves her." It sounds crazy even writing it out, just TOXIC. For a lot of us, this sounds crazy to read, but there are parts in us that have accepted pieces of Yvette's story as being okay!

This "code" is about shifting mindsets, and if we're going to change the narrative in all areas of our lives, we have to tackle the unhealthy ones we have allowed. Let me be clear, cheating is not normal and not something you should be allowing under the guise of love. Also, we understand the Bibles principle on forgiveness and marriages, catch that key word "marriage." It will require a lot of, but cheating should be given a pass for disrespect. In all relationships, each party is maturing forgiveness, but that does not mean you accept anything. Can I be honest with you? There are some things I accepted because I figured it was love. I've shared before when I was a teenager in one of my relationships, I experienced some domestic abuse. The first time it happened it was exactly like the scene from baby boy where Jody smacked Yvette. I remember it so vividly. I was so in shock I don't remember saying anything, like my jaw dropped and that movie scene flashed in my head, "You said you'd never hit me Jody" is what I was thinking. I didn't leave nor did I tell him to leave my house. I feel I accepted it because I figured that was love. As someone who is naturally a protector and a southside saint who fights, I can't even fathom allowing that now.

We have allowed society, movies, and what we did not see growing up to dictate what we will accept, instead of seeing ourselves as a new creation. I could easily still think toxicity is acceptable, but as I grew up my mindset began to shift. Can we go even deeper? A part of being honest with yourself and shifting your mindset is realizing that you can be toxic too. I have to say it. We have to stop putting the blame only on men like us women don't have toxic traits, too. Let's get into these unhealthy expectations we put on men. First, when you get married, your husband is not your father. Some women have this "savior" expectation, but our husbands can never replace Jesus and was not meant to save us. Our future spouses are not meant to become our idol or "god." At the end of the day, God is a jealous God, and that will not change because God presented us to one of His fine saved sons. Settling is so much more than connecting with something less than you desire. How many times do we settle within ourselves? We allow our mindsets to remain the same, and we don't reach our own maximum potential. Yep, maybe you aren't just settling in your romantic relationship, or maybe you're settling with living in a lesser version of yourself. There is hope, not only our lasting hope in the cross, but a hope that we can change our narratives by being renewed through the word of truth, the Bible. Too many times, I personally believe we forget how the Bible is purposeful in all areas-- sex, friendships, hurt, our minds, and so much more; even after salvation, understanding that we are relational beings. God gives us wisdom and instructions on how to navigate life while were here. We can be so guarded to protect ourselves that we end up doing more harm. We will end up much older one day and realize we never allowed the word of God to heal us internally. We kept so much bottled in that we completely missed the beauty of this life and the opportunities that could have brought us much joy. I want you to leave this book being free in your mind! I want you to leave this book being so courageous to accept the liberty in Christ, liberty from the bondage of sin, and the grace to get back up again.

Grace is such a powerful thing, and I want you to fully accept God's grace in your healing! As someone whose main pursuit is to "keep the main thing, the main thing," which is to be gospel centered, I want you to understand how this is not a self-centered task. Although you are intentional about doing this work, this is so much bigger than you. This work will further how you love your neighbor, how you walk in the spirit and what comes out of your mouth – because if we're honest, if you're saved, we still have areas in our lives where we need to walk in the spirit more and not the flesh. Let's get into some scriptures, the Bible says, "It's not what goes in a man that defiles him, but that which comes out" (Matthew 15:11). The book of Galatians chapter 5 states, "The works of the flesh are evident: sensuality, idolatry, impurity, sexual immorality, sorcery, enmity, strife, jealousy, fits of anger, rivalries, dissensions, divisions, envy, drunkenness, orgies, and things like these." Now, as believers and even in relationships, horizontally most people can say that there are areas named above in our flesh that need to be walked out differently. The New Testament tells us we showcase our love for God by following his commandments—"Love God with our whole heart, mind, soul, and strength, and the second is to love our neighbor as ourself" (Matthew 22:37).

When our minds are renewed with the word of God, our hearts are shifted, and we will walk in the spirit and not the flesh. We will not be allowing our unhealed parts to cause us to operate in envy, fits of anger, strife, etc. If we are honest with ourselves, a lot of what we do is from a broken place. Our scars speak loud. For some of us not seeing healthy marriages or marriages at all for that matter have shaped our expectations! Growing up in a single parent home was shaping my expectations in so many ways. The crazy thing is that when I was a teenager, I never saw myself being a single parent, like it never crossed my mind, yet I had these tainted views and thought divorce was acceptable.

Can I be vulnerable and share with you something the Lord showed me about myself a few years ago? I'm a runner. I will never forget that moment. I was driving on the freeway to pick my mom up from work, and God came in and had me edgeless by the time I got to her job. I actually have it recorded on video. When things would get hard or I would have an argument with someone, my first reaction was to RUN! Yes, this is still about marriages and how it trickled over to relationships with family members. You see for me, having kids with someone was always the ultimate sign of commitment, not marriage—again because I was a "runner." In my mind once I got married, if anything ever went left and I needed to leave with no connection, I could. I had been setting myself up for divorce and a way out my whole life. I am the type of person who would start over completely. I could literally forget a person ever existed. It wasn't like I would see you in public and feel some way. No matter how long the relationship, I could block out any memories of us in my mind because I never opened myself up fully anyway. I used to imagine myself as the person who would move to a different state and start completely over, unlike the women in the movies who wanted to keep the house, sleeping in the bed they used to sleep in with their spouse while he was living his best life in a new condo with a new chick. Nope. I always said I would be in the man's position and forget everything –that goes back to my last point, of why I equated having kids with being the ultimate sign of commitment and not marriage, because I knew once I had kids with someone I was trapped forever.

I could not just escape into my new life of bliss and forget about my future spouse because I would have some form of attachment to them forever as I looked at our child. There would always be a reminder of us that I couldn't escape. I could not just up and run. You see, God showed me this year's ago, unlocking so many layers of myself that I did not know were broken. Now, I had no intentions of this being the direction God led me to write my code on, but hey I guess he needs somebody to hear this so they can truly heal. While we are here, let me throw it out there that healing mentally is a daily choice! I never want to paint the picture that I have it all together; renewing your mind is a daily choice. When Satan tempted Jesus in the wilderness the Bible tells us, "He departed from him until an opportune time" (Luke 4: 13). It would be foolish to think that Satan will not try to take you back to your old ways of thinking or present you with opportunities to choose. When he does present things to me or there are seasons when I need more strength, I have to still be diligent to not allow rejection or any other area to speak FOR me, but instead I speak to those things with the word of God! During that season, I had a vision, and it has stuck with me ever since. In the vision, I saw me and my future husband in our house, and we got into a disagreement. I remember my brokenness speaking for me, and I went to the other room and started packing my stuff to leave. You see, my response was to RUN! Now, I'm not married or dating at the moment I'm writing this, but my husband had the most gentle, patient and loving spirit I've ever encountered. I could feel his love and long suffering for me even in that vision, like he never questioned or thought about leaving, and I was already planning my exit over something small. In the vision, I was calculating in my mind to forget about him, but as I was walking around gathering stuff, he came and asked me, "What is for dinner?" in the gentlest tone, and I broke down crying! In the vision, I was confused that he was even asking that question. I thought to myself, "The audacity." Then, I realized how quickly I run out of fear of getting hurt and my heart broke!

You see, I thought forgetting was easier than forgiving, communicating and reconciling! I know I'm not alone, and I don't want you to go through life operating from that broken space. Although it was a vision, I know God was showing me what was still lingering in me that needed to be healed. This goes back to my point that sometimes it's not always the men. How many of us operate from hurt or rejection? For instance, we can be the most faithful and dope women ever, but our constant nagging can be toxic as well! The Bible tells us, "It's better to live in a corner of a housetop than in a house shared with a quarrelsome wife" (Proverbs 25:24).

Our nagging and attitudes can be toxic. Just as we believe we deserve to be treated a certain way, our future spouses that are also made in the image of God deserve respect and love as well! God designed marriage between man and woman, and we see the beauty of that covenant as Christ is the head of the church and we are his bride! Some of you are purposed by God to be married. Although marriage will be a reflection of Christ, and there will be much healing that will take place between you two, you can also take some initiative to grow now! I no longer want divorce to be my go-to as an escape. I desire a happy, more importantly, a healthy marriage where we always choose each other.

I don't know why writing this section has me so emotional, but we have to talk about this! Let's go straight in. God is not like man! For some of you, you may have just said, "Well duh, Jasmine, we know that." But do you really? If we are shifting unhealthy mindsets, the foundation of that has to be how we view God. If God and his word must be the foundation for which all of our unhealthy mindsets change, we must tackle our unhealthy views of God!

Many of us struggle with Seeing God as ABBA father because we did not have our fathers growing up or we had difficult relationships with our parents! We have a hard time going to God asking him for anything, because we believe he won't come through, how we've had in the past with expectations from our parents! As an adult, you don't realize how these subtle things from your childhood and what was absent is now having an effect on your spiritual relationship. How many of us only see God as a "punisher?" We mess up, or we are doing a little better in life and waiting for God to drop the ball! We mess up and equate our suffering as repercussions solely. We see "good" as "bad" subconsciously and that unhealthy view of him as someone who comes in to take away what is going well.

Not only do believers do this, even though God has proven himself time and time again, we still don't see him as GOOD! We even see people who don't believe in God do this—people will claim that they are atheist all day and believe in a "higher power," yet when something tragic in the world happens, they automatically question, "Why would God let this happen?" I remember a few months after I got saved. I was on my way to a guest church service, and we got into a car accident. I remember standing on the side of the road so upset thinking, "I've been living for you, and you let this happen." I was so upset I could cry because I equated anything bad to God! I couldn't fully grasp that we will endure suffering, even as Christians, and no that fender bender was not God punishing me for something.

We don't really believe all things are working together for our good as the book of Romans tells us. If we did, we would see our circumstances in light of Gods perfect wisdom and love. When we learn God's character, we can trust his heart, even when we don't understand! In shifting our mindsets, we must be honest that we couldn't fully believe all of God's word because we don't really trust him! We don't fully see him as good, and yes, it is something that is learned. I've been walking with God for eight years now, and I still have moments where I have to remind myself of all the times God carried me over life's adversities and came through. There are seasons where I don't see Gods goodness until that hard season is over and I'm looking back, again learned.

Too many times we think we are wiser than God. I don't think we do it intentionally, but life makes us believe we are stronger than we are. God is the only one that is all knowing and everywhere at once—The Bible tells us, "He knows our going down and our sitting up. He knows the number of hairs on our head" (Psalms 139:2). Basically, God has kept you. Even in his wisdom and knowing everything about you, He still sent his son to die for our sins! He knew the worst about us before we were, and he still sent us the best of Him—himself in flesh. Even writing this, I'm reminded of how good God is! How could someone be deemed bad, when from the beginning they had us in mind to redeem us! God is so good that He has always had our eternity in mind. We get so caught up on this earth, not realizing the best in eternity is really yet to come. He was good before we could grasp it, and he will be good when we take our last breath. I hope this reassured you as you strive to grow—you cannot shift and grow with a word you don't truly believe from an author that is good or correct. When God speaks something, he tells us fore knowing the outcome already. He tells us understanding that we will still need grace to carry us through the process. He leads us by still waters being the captain of the ship.

The necessity for this book is not simply to showcase a collective of amazing authors, but it is an example of GIRL CODE lived out! As you read this manual, you are reading the testimonies of women who overcame and are still overcoming. This is not a "I have it all together" book, but God has it all together. Healing is not easy. Shifting is not easy. Letting go of the very ways that led you for decades is not easy—it is a process, but the beautiful part is that it's a process, not being walked alone. My dear sister. God is with you.

No matter where you find yourself in this book, I don't ever want someone to leave a moment with me feeling condemned because you may still be here mentally. What I will say is that you don't have to stay THERE! Not only have we prayed over whoever may be reading this, we have fasted and sought God that these words would penetrate who it was intended for. The gospel is truly the only thing that saves, but we overcome by the blood of the lamb and the words of our testimonies—there is strength in sharing our stories and pointing you right back to Jesus!

I want you to set this book down at the end and understand the finished work of Jesus. I want you to see everything you have ever searched for was laid at the foot of the cross! Coming from someone who was selling her body briefly and had to change a whole lot of mindsets even after I got saved. Guess what? Grace kept me, and it is keeping you! Galatians tells us, "God is working in us to will and do his good pleasure" (Philippians 2:13). Keep pressing towards the mark, sisters, and know that if you are adopted into the kingdom, you are in the hands of the creator and not the created. In those hands, you will never fall. SHIFT!

Questions for the Journey:

Which areas in my life are God calling me to be renewed?

What caused these mindsets in the first place?

What unhealthy mindsets about God need to be shifted?

What scriptures will you meditate on to remind you of God's goodness?

Write out why you believe God is good?

Prayer for yourself:

_____
_____
_____
_____
_____
_____
_____
_____
_____
_____
_____
_____
_____
_____
_____
_____
_____
_____
_____
_____

Receiving God's Love
By: Teairra Barnes

The love code is a very important code to maintain as you journey through life. The Bible tells us it is the greatest code of them all. In fact, the word tells us that many things will die off, but love will never fail (1 Corinthians 13:8). During the hardest times in history, if love was at the forefront and implemented whole heartedly, then the world would truly be a better place. Love has covered a multitude of sins in my life, as well as in other's lives, when they allowed love to conquer. To reap the benefits of love, I truly believe you have to receive God's love first. In return, you will be able to reciprocate the grace God has given you to others.

There are different types of love. The types of love are Agape (Unconditional love), Eros (Romantic Love), Philia (Affectionate Love), Philautia (self-love), Storge (Familiar Love), Pragma (Enduring Love), Ludus (Playful Love), Mania (Obsessive love). Agape is the foundation of how each relationship should start, God's love. Agape love may grow into different levels of love. However, I am certain if you know and feel God's agape love, you will be able to place the correct boundaries with each type of love. Let's walk through how to accept God's love. In return, we can be love. God's love is a promise that he gives to us, no matter if we want it or not.

First, before we can even receive God's love, we need to truly understand the meaning.
Webster's Dictionary tells us that love (noun) is an intense feeling of deep affection. Many may be able to relate to the powerful feeling as butterflies,

nervousness, peace, emotion overload, joy, happiness. There are so many different emotions felt when you give or receive love. It's powerful. Webster also gives a verb definition for love. It is an action which needs to take place. It's something that a person can do. In fact, we must show love in the world, everyone needs it. The verb definition of love is to like or enjoy very much. We must be women who give the world agape love.

A few years ago, I struggled with the meaning of love. Being kind is cool, but come on, we know people take advantage of that. I became uneasy with just loving people because it was "the right thing to do". I wanted to know why it was something I had to do. God placed, now one of my favorite scriptures, in my spirit to show me why. He loves us so much that he will show us why love will never fail and is the greatest of them all. In 1 Corinthians 3-13, it states, "If I give all my possessions to feed the poor, and if I surrender my body to be burned but do not have love, it does me no good at all. Love endures with patience and serenity. Love is kind and thoughtful and is not jealous or envious; love does not brag and is not proud or arrogant. It is not rude nor self-seeking. It is not provoked nor overly sensitive and easily angered. Love does not take into account a wrong endured. It does not rejoice at injustice but rejoices with the truth [when right and truth prevail]. Love bears all things [regardless of what comes], believes all things [regardless of what comes], believes all things [looking for the best in each one], hopes all things [remaining steadfast during difficult times], endures all things [without weakening]. Love never fails [it never fades nor ends]. But as for prophecies, they will cease; as for the gift of special knowledge, it will pass away. For we know in part and we prophesy in part [for our knowledge is fragmentary and incomplete]. But when that which is complete and perfect comes, that which is incomplete and partial will pass away. When I was a child, I talked like a child, I thought like a child, I reasoned like a child. When I became a man, I did away with childish things. For now, [in this time of imperfection] we see in a mirror dimly [a blurred reflection, a riddle, an enigma], but then [when the time of perfection comes, we will see reality] face to face. Now I know in part [just in fragments], but then I will know fully, just as I have been fully known [by God]. And now there remain: faith, [abiding trust in God and his promises], hope [confident expectation of eternal salvation], love [unselfish love for others growing out of God's love for me], these three [the choicest graces]; but the greatest of these is love." In order to recognize something, we must be made aware of it. Always know what love is. Once you understand it, you will be able to know what type of love should be displayed to the people in your life. If there is ever a time where you need to see if love is being conveyed, replace the name of the act/person with love. If it lacks anything, it may be an area that needs God's love to cover.

When we know what love is, we can receive and acknowledge God's love. We can even be patient and acknowledge our emotions and see if they are the truth, the real deal of what God says love is. I begin to think of God's love as a relationship between a newborn/child and their parent. A parent will do anything for their child. Our father feels the same way about us. A newborn doesn't have any control over where they are placed, who their parents are, when they will be placed in the world, not even the time they are born. They have absolutely no control over their existence and what they are called to. However, God is omniscient. Nothing will surprise him. We don't have a say so on many things that happened in our lives, yet we are called to do life on Earth and to do it well, God being one who makes no mistakes. If we have received his love, we know his love won't fail. God's plan is never to harm us but to prosper us, so we know it will work out for our good. In this comparison, the mother being what God is ALWAYS and even more to his children. God knows how to love us and care for us better than anyone else. He gives us what we need before we can even have an idea of the lack. Similar to when a baby begins to cry, and the mother may produce milk due to the hormones it triggers.

Mothers are gifted; the mother's instinct is to be able to know exactly what that child will need. As the Lord knows and makes everything perfect, a mother's love for her child will allow her to make sacrifices for her child to have the best. God is way better than that. He sacrificed his son so that we could always be loved by him and have eternal life (John 3:16). Now, that is love.

Imagine knowing that your child is innocent and is being nailed to the cross for others. Could you be called to this mission and trust the plan was working for good? When a child is being birthed by a woman, her cervix opens up to accommodate the baby passing through. Her body was made to carry the child.

The mother's body was made perfect for that child to be birthed the way it should be. That is the same with God's idea of why he birthed us. He knew the purpose would ease the pain that we would have to endure. When he breathed life into you, he came with a mindset bigger than the process. He knew once we received his love that we could conquer what he put us here for. Love will cast out fear and doubt (1 John 4:18). God knows what we are capable of and what we are not, even as a mother can tell you what her child is capable of the majority of the time. When a child is sick, scared, uneasy, or having any discomfort, the mother is able to recognize the problem and give them the peace and comfort to ease the discomfort. This is the same when we receive God's love. The difficult emotions are easier to bear. Studies show that the newborn will recognize their mother's voice first, as she carried the baby for 9 months. With God's love, it is the same way we will be able to recognize his voice. John 10:27 says, "The sheep that are MY own hear my voice and listen to me; I know them, and they follow me. It will be things that no one taught you and maybe ways that were taught to you wrongfully that God will speak to you about and help you change. He may have brought you in the way he did through your mother, but he will still raise you up when we receive His love. When a child begins to grow, the mother's responsibility is to show the child the right way to go (Proverbs 22:6). This is the same with God's love for his children. He corrects, guides, and teaches his children right from wrong, only if his children can receive the correction as love. When you haven't received God's love, you'll take correction as being unloved. You'll continue to allow the correction to bring you the complete opposite of God's plan and love. Rather than knowing that God's love is everything, sin will bring you to a place where You can't receive correction if you aren't looking at it from a love perspective but as a disorder. No matter what, God's love will never fail.

Whatever God allows to happen, his love is in it. There is nothing that happens bad in our lives that God has not given authority to happen. If he gave authority for it to happen, he knew you could overcome the strongholds and pain attached to it. As a mother and child grows, there will be things that bring discomfort and disorder, growing pains, but if love is placed in the relationship, they will eventually appreciate the process, the same with God and his love for us. Even if we need pruning, healing, or understanding, our relationship with

God won't cease. He will never leave nor forsake us (Deuteronomy 31: 6). When we receive God's love, it covers a multitude of sins. It allows us to stand boldly and powerful in this world and know that love conquers. God's love is unconditional. As a child is taken care of by a mother and has no worries, we shouldn't either. We don't have to do anything to receive his love; it is a promise to us. God can do far more than any person.

Now that we can identify love and know that nothing can stop us from receiving His love, let's talk about how we should place the love God has given us back in the world. When you accept this unconditional love, accepting and loving the world comes easier. When you were in the process of receiving and accepting God's love, I am certain he took you through a growth process, similar to being raised. He showed you why you are here, your purpose. He is now raising you to walk boldly in your identity daily. You can deal with your assignments you are called to with grace and mercy, just like He did with you. You begin to know what battles to go to war in and which ones you aren't called to. You also begin to love others as he loves you. Yes, even the ones who have hurt you. You begin to realize God is not a respecter of persons. The same God who loves you loves the individual who may have hurt you. The same God who loves you loves everybody, no matter what sin they've committed. No sin is greater than another, not one. Luke 6:37 says, "Judge not, and you will not be judged; condemn not, and you will not be condemned; forgive, and you will be forgiven."

At some point, you begin to realize, "I can't ask God to forgive me if I can't forgive others." If he forgave your deepest darkest sin and loved you through it, he would do the same for the next person. The God who calls you by name has hidden riches in your suffering and darkness. When you receive God's love, you begin to be patient and seek his face on how to deal with every situation. You're able to acknowledge your emotions but act on what you know to be true, God's love. God didn't make a mistake with our emotions, but remember love is greater, so you begin to allow love to trump all emotions.

As you have already decoded a few girl codes, know that spiritual welfare is one of God's first missions for your life. Before he knew whose womb he would form you in, he knew the battle you were called to defeat and why you had to go to the bloodline he would place you in. To spread the light and love we should always remember that he placed you there for a time such as this. You might endure some pain, but His love should bring peace for the mission, peace that surpasses all understanding. Even when God is doing a great work, there will be shaking. Be patient until God's love is shown in every area of the matter. Everything is a process, but don't allow what you see to stop you from what you now know, God's love, which will conquer.

Love is many things, but it is never deceitful. Nothing toxic comes from genuine love. I'm not saying he won't call you to painful situations, but if he calls you to it, he will equip you for it. He will get the glory, and his love can fix anything. Nothing is impossible for him. The enemy's trick is to have us feeling as though we can't overcome the pain, that God doesn't love us. He even begins to have us walking in discouragement, doubt, guilt, and sorrow. Yes, the pain is real. We may have to go through a lot to heal, but if God allows it, he will provide an escape. He will keep nothing from you. He will have people pour into you. He will give you instructions on how to heal. It may even be that he takes you through an extensive healing process. I do know that the pain has purpose, and your healing is your responsibility. What you endured wasn't just about you. If you allow God's love to overshadow the matter, you will see that it wasn't just about you. Your testimony will help many. Love will conquer! I encourage you to walk boldly in love, allow it to be the foundation in everything you do. Be patient with everyone. You never know the battle they may be fighting. Be kind always. Don't boast. Remember, it's not about you. Stay humble, sweetheart. That is the only way you will be able to give agape love. If not, you will fall short with thinking it was you. Don't get angry too quick. That's where the heart will deceive you. That is where the trick of the enemy resides. Don't count the wrongs but the blessings. We all fall short of the glory of God, but love covers a multitude of sins. Always be quick to help your sister with things of truth, and don't spend too much time on evil. Acknowledge the changes that need to happen, but don't allow the enemy more time in the ring than he needs. Remember, he is already defeated. Love protects, always trusts, always hopes, and always preserves. Agape love will bless the universe. Start off small and show yourself grace but begin to pour love back out.

Questions to consider:
1. What's the worst thing in your life presently you never believed you could heal from?
2. When was the first time you felt God's love?
3. What is Love to you?
4. Would you rather have love or loyalty?

Purpose Moves: Obedience

By: Tiffany Lindsey

Shortly after graduating high school, I attended a technical school. All my life I had loved animals, I was always curious about the similarities and differences between them all, although through high school, I wanted to do and become several different things. At one point, I wanted to be a fashion designer, a business owner, and even a teacher. Honestly, even though I had thought of several different careers for myself, I didn't come up with a decision until months before my senior year of high school ended. Due to that, I made the decision to go to school to be a Veterinary Technician, a nurse for animals. I went in for an interview with admissions and got a call that I was accepted within a few days. While I was in tech school, I found myself pregnant.

Due to being pregnant, there was a time I thought I would no longer be able to attend because of the nature of work that I was and would be doing. The use of radiology and working around larger animals made it almost impossible for me. Fortunately, I was able to continue attending school while taking the necessary precautions. I went through school attending classes and missing little to no days throughout each semester. I was determined this was not only what I wanted to do, but it was what I was going to do. After eighteen months, I graduated. Within a few months, I had given birth to my daughter and went on maternity leave.

Since I was on maternity leave, my externship was on hold until I came back. After it ended, I went on my externship. It was interesting being in the field outside of my comfort zone. Don't get me wrong, at school, we had a lot of hands-on experiences, from learning basic kennel duties, to knowing the anatomy of different animals, and treating them as needed. The experience was there. This time it was different; I knew none of the people that I was now working with, and I didn't know any of the animals. Nevertheless, I eventually came to know everyone, including some of the animals that came to our clinic. It was a process between working and becoming a new mom, but I completed my externship and soon began to look for a job at an animal clinic. I called several places and went on several interviews, eager to start my new career. Eventually, I was hired to work at a clinic that took exotic animals, along with dogs and cats. To be completely honest, I loved animals, but I did not love where I was or what I had to do. It was surely an adventure, regardless of how confident I did or didn't feel. I got the chance to work with sugar gliders, guinea pigs, a chameleon and an opossum. Yes, I said an opossum! Lol! You would think because I went to school that I should have decided or at least known the things that would be required of me as a veterinary technician. I did actually. I knew things would be slightly different when I got out there and was no longer in school, but I knew what was expected of me and what I needed to do. Being a new mom while also fully starting a career that I knew I would be in for the rest of my life took some adjusting to, but I adjusted. If only I had known that I would be learning to make even more adjustments. I and my daughter's father had broken up, and I had gotten to a place where I no longer wanted to know of Jesus but to actually know him.

> I no longer wanted religion. I wanted a relationship. Soon after the break-up, I found myself being a single mom. I never wanted to be a single mom, but then again how many of us want to. I never thought I would first become a mom before ever having a wedding and becoming married, but I did. I never saw my daughter's father and I breaking up, but everything happens for a reason. I didn't see it then and there when everything was fresh, but months later, not even years later, I would come to understand why. Just like I was learning to adjust before, I found myself adjusting again. I was not thriving, but surviving, and at the same time building my relationship with God.

I began to read my Bible more, praying more and serving more. Slowly, but surely my faith began to grow and because I was spending more time with God, I began to hear him more. I had connected with like-minded individuals to fellowship with. Also, I had become more intentional. I took the time whenever I could to commune with God. If it meant me waking up early in the morning, I did it. If it meant having quiet time whenever I could, I did it. I didn't always get it right, but I tried and eventually I did. I continued working at the animal clinic. As the months went on, I had a feeling that I would later understand as I was being led. The more I worked, the more uncomfortable I became. I became less confident that was where I was supposed to be. I can't remember exactly where I was, but I had clearly heard to start looking for a job. I thought to myself, "Okay, no problem." However, I heard, "Don't just look for another job, but look for a new job where you will be working with children." Pause, wait what? I didn't get it, and I struggled for a long time wondering two things. The first thing I was wondering was if I had heard God clearly...I had doubts. The second thing I wondered was if it even made sense to do this, if I was hearing correctly. I had gone to school, endured debt from student loans, but was now going to do something I had no experience in doing or no education in whatsoever.

After praying and seeking God, I had decided that I was going to trust and chose to be obedient. I didn't know the why, how or when. All I knew was what I was supposed to do. We had a rotating schedule at work with off days in between. On my off days, I made calls, filled out applications, and went on interviews. I went on about five different interviews and eventually went on what would be my last for a while. I had continued going to work as usual until I was called into my bosses' office. I was told that I was not meeting their expectations and that they were letting me go. I had not worked in many places before there, but I had never been fired. I began to question myself and felt guilty like I was a bad person for being let go.

Those emotions were short lived as I remembered what God said. I took my belongings, said my goodbyes and walked out the door to my car. I had called my mom and told her what happened. She was sad and disappointed, but she already knew I had been looking for another job. I figured that with the time I had now I would be able to go on more interviews.

Unbeknownst to me, three days after getting fired, I would be hired and already starting my first job working with children. A few days before getting fired I had gone on one particular interview. I had done two parts of that interview. The first part was me answering questions...the usual. The second part was a working interview. This part of the interview was where they would see me in action working with the children. I'm not going to lie; I was nervous. I had never worked with any children besides my own daughter. I had no idea how they would react to me or how I would even interact with them without it being awkward and forced. Surprisingly, nothing felt forced, and slowly but surely, they warmed up to me.

Before leaving, I was told, "Due to other applicants applying, you will be hearing a decision from us within a few days." I left there not knowing what to expect. I left there not knowing what my potential employers thought of what I had said and done at the interview. After waiting and praying, praying and waiting, I got the call and was offered the job. Years later, I am now where I am today. Being at that first job, I learned so much about working with children. The school was Reggio Emilia philosophy based. Instead of the teachers leading everything, the children did, as it was child led. I was pulled out of my comfort zone, as what I thought learning was supposed to look like, looked completely different. I gained confidence and experience knowing that I could work with children. Not only could I work with children, but I was actually good at it. I have also had the opportunity to work at a charter school. I knew the areas I worked in had a stigma, but I felt the need to be there. That job, like all the others, helped develop me as a person. Where some people would have never stepped in, I went in. It wasn't easy. I had moments where I questioned if I was supposed to be there because of different things that were happening. All in all, I learned something. Although children may have different backgrounds, they all need the same thing. They may look different, talk different and even live differently, but they all want to feel needed. I didn't think things could be any more challenging until I went to my next job, a non-profit.

As individuals, I truly believe there are jobs we take, and then they are jobs that are given to us. The job working at a homeless shelter was given. Not only was it a homeless shelter, but it was Christian based. Being there, I got the chance to see so many different things from a different perspective. There were many things when it came to homeless people that were either wrong or just all the way off. I wasn't sure. It's one thing to be driving in your car and seeing someone stand on the side of the road who is homeless. It's another thing when you are working with that population and helping families. While working there, I had grown deeper in my relationship with Christ. I had to. With the amount of warfare, you could not just go in there open. I could not get prepared, I had to stay prepared. From parents, who themselves grew up homeless, to children who had been in positions where they had been abused, you never knew anyone's story unless you took the time to listen.

Being there built me emotionally, mentally, but most of all spiritually. I will always remember that season being a time that I would no longer be the same. I left there more prepared as I would begin to work with another population. I had now felt confident enough working with children, a lot more confident than when I had first started years before. I had worked with children of different ethnicities and backgrounds. I had worked with children who had homes and those who were waiting for their own. I was now on a new journey working with children that had ASD, autism spectrum disorder. If you know anything about ASD, you get it. If you don't, there is a wide spectrum that people who have been diagnosed can fall within, hence the word spectrum. It took a lot of training and even certification, might I add, to be there. It was all necessary though. You cannot work with children who have ASD without knowing what it is and what it can look like for different children. Not only that, being a behavior therapist, I had to learn and know how to go about working with each child. It was a process as everything is, but it was something that opened my eyes even more. I became more knowledgeable. Instead of not understanding like I didn't before, I began to understand. I did more than understand though; I began to embrace.

Little did I know, I would be needing that experience later on in life. After that, I had my own classroom in a preschool working with two-year-old's. Let me just say, there was never a dull moment! If you are a parent or have been around nieces and nephews or just any child around that age, you get where I'm coming from. Lol! Being there, I learned to create my own lesson plans for my students to have throughout the day. It was also an interesting time helping to potty train my class. There were many moments of laughter, creativity and fun! One reason I always enjoyed working with children was because you could be yourself and you would not get judged.

> There were a few times during holiday breaks that I was asked to step in for a few minutes with the after schoolers while my children were having their nap time. I'm telling you I truly believe that each job was preparation for the next. I was nervous being with the older children because I had heard how some of them could be, but surprisingly it went a lot better than I expected. Fast forward and guess what my next job was, working in an afterschool program. I was still nervous but felt slightly more confident working with older children. There I had to adapt my language as I realized that obviously the way you would talk to a two-year-old and an almost twelve-year-old are completely different. While being there, I also had a student who was autistic. My co-teacher had told me that me working there was the first time she had seen him interacting with someone the way that he had interacted with me. I was humbled and then thought of the experience that I had previously being an ABA therapist working with children that had ASD.

I later began working at a public school in a Read 180 classroom, a part of Special Education. I was now working with middle school students. It's amazing how that went because I had been trying to work in that specific school district for years. I had attended there as a student and really wanted to be able to give back to students who were there now. Honestly, I had no idea what to expect being there. These children were older, and I blended in, as far as size, with many of them. I wondered if that would be a problem as far as how they would view me. I did not want them to view me as a peer, but as an adult, an educator. My mind was blown on so many levels. There were connections made with students that still continue to this day. I have been the person different students said hello to every chance they got. In other instances, I have been the one that they could confide in. My life will never be the same. Understanding children who are in middle school has opened up my eyes to a stage in life that I had long forgotten.

As much as I went there to make an impact in their lives, they, every single one of them, made an impact in mine.

> Every now and then, I would wonder if I had just gone to school to get a degree to be a teacher, would I be where I am now or had the experiences I've had. Would I have gotten the chance to work with younger children besides my own? Would I have gotten the chance to work in special education? Would I be the same person I am now, then? I don't know, only God knows. Maybe the answer to every single question is yes. Maybe the answer to every single question is no. The feelings I had over ten years ago about leaving my chosen profession have changed. I didn't get it then, but I think, no I believe, I have it now. As people, we want what we want. We have dreams, goals, and visions. Don't get me wrong, there is nothing wrong with that. These things are good to have as it gives you something to work towards, to look forward to. However, God knows everything! He created us for a purpose. We are not individuals just wandering around aimlessly. We are not here to just be here. Me, you, your family and your friends, the people you know and the people you don't know, are here for a purpose. Many of us don't know right away, some do. However, you learn. Regardless of how you find out, you find out. Once you know it, you know it. Now, there is free will. You can choose to embrace your purpose or ignore it, that's up to you. In my case, I didn't know my purpose. I just knew I liked what I liked. I had decided to make a career out of what I thought was best for me. I never really considered anything else but that. It took a lot for me to get here, but I made a choice. I chose to listen to God and be obedient. As I stated before, I had no idea what the what or why was. I was scared, and I had doubt. I was familiar with what I knew, but I moved. I moved in obedience, trusting that even if I did not have it figured out, God did.

I'm not saying that operating in your purpose will be easy. Chances are that doing so will not be easy, but it does not mean that it is not worth it. Can you imagine what things would have been like if I chose to work with animals? Would I have worked at another clinic only to possibly be fired? Would I have eventually grown confident enough and stayed where I was, never moving beyond where I was? I don't know, but I've learned that instead of questioning everything when it comes to God, just say yes when it comes to something that He is requiring of you. Someone else could have taken my place and met all the people I have met. Someone else could have been where I was. However, it wasn't another person that met the people I have met. It wasn't another person that was where I was. I was there, I was. I said yes, and I'm so glad about it! My life has changed, and I know that many children's lives were changed as well. I know my purpose. It may not be popular, and I may have not chosen it, but I was chosen and for that I am eternally grateful.

I hope what I shared resonates with you. It took me one yes for me to know what my purpose is, but it took obedience for me to walk in that purpose throughout the years. I have a few questions for you to answer. Some of these questions you may be able to answer right away. Some of these questions may cause you to think for a while in order for you to answer them. Either way is fine with me. What I want more than anything is for you to be honest with yourself and honest with the answers that you have for these questions. I won't see the answers. Truthfully, no one may ever know the answers but you and God unless you share them with someone else. If you're currently in a career or doing something that you like, but you are unsure about. If you've been feeling led to go in a different direction like me, but you don't really want to because you've invested so much time and or money into what you're already doing, consider what I have shared. If you're doubting yourself about making that move because you are afraid of what others may say or think about what you do, don't worry about it.

It's easy to say don't worry about it, but like many things it's not easily done. I get it; trust me, I do. It's in this time where you have to know and understand what's more important. It's in this time that you have to understand, "Who exactly are you trying to please?" Everybody won't get it. Some people may look at you sideways. Some people may smile in your face but talk about you later to someone else. Some people may even stop talking to you altogether because of your obedience. Let me tell you this, it's not for them to get. God didn't tell whatever He told you to your mother, sister, friend, or even your spouse. He said what He said to you, and it's up to you to listen and move in purpose or to ignore it. I can't choose for you, only you can. I would hope that even despite the questions, fears and doubts that you may have that you would say yes. You deserve to live life on purpose with the purpose that God has given you. There are lives that you will impact, but you may never see it if you choose not to be obedient. When you choose, make sure you choose wisely.

Questions to think about:

1. What does purpose mean to you?
2. What does obedience look like to you?
3. Is it more important to do what you want to do or what God wants you to do? Why?
4. Do you believe that what you do and don't do has a direct impact on the lives of others?
5. If you know your purpose, what is it, and how have you walked in
1. in it so far?

If you're like me, some of these questions may have been a breeze for you to answer. If you're also like me, some of these may have been difficult for you. In some cases, you may have left one or two unanswered and that's okay. I'd rather you take your time and have some questions unanswered than to rush and put whatever, just to say that you have gotten it done. That's not what this is about. Whatever questions you had trouble answering or have yet to answer, I know someone who does have them, God. I've learned so far that when I don't know the answer He does, ask Him.

Scarred for Purpose

By: MoNique Perkins

What is purpose? The Oxford Dictionary defines purpose as the reason for which something is done or created or for which something exists. Now, I ask, what is your purpose? Why are you here? What was God's intent when he allowed you to grace this world with your presence? Once that specific thing is realized, life begins to make sense. Every person God has created has a divine purpose that will specifically bring God a unique Glory. Oftentimes, many of us stumble through life trying to figure out that specific thing. Sadly enough, some people will leave this earth never knowing what it feels like to fulfill their purpose. There is a quote by Les Brown that says, "The graveyard is the richest place on earth because it is here that you will find all the hopes and dreams that were never fulfilled, the books that were never written, the songs that were never sung, the inventions that were never shared, the cures that were never discovered, all because someone was too afraid to take the first step, keep with the problem or determined to carry out their dream."

God does not do anything by happenstance. Everything from the smallest molecule to the largest planet in the Solar System has a divine purpose to bring God glory. The Bible states in Isaiah 43:7 KJV, "Even everyone that is called by my name: for I have created him for my glory, I have formed him; yea, I have made him." The greatest gift you can give to God is to completely walk out his intent for your life. That is what glorifying God really looks like. The problem is most people have no issue with the glory part, but they refuse to go through the necessary processes that produce it. Some of the greatest elevations come after the most intense battles you have ever endured. Pain births purpose, and purpose positions you for glory.

If I told you my journey to discovering my purpose was a walk in the park, I would be lying. There was nothing easy about it. My journey was filled with tears, heartache, and abuse that seemed to come consistently in every season of my life. It was as if I could not catch a break. Purpose was the furthest thing from my mind, and I only saw myself as a victim. Enduring years of sexual and physical abuse as a child created a void in me that I believed nothing could fill. I went through the motions, just doing enough to get by. When I found myself dreaming of a better reality, my past would creep in, reminding me that I was not adequate to do anything. Pain was dictating my life. Because I did not understand how to use pain to my advantage, I allowed it to win. I was the greatest friend and encourager to everyone else, but I never had one good thing to say about myself. I was consistent about helping others launch and grow their vision, but I would sabotage my own because I believed it had no value. This was my reality. With each passing year, I was becoming more frustrated and unsatisfied. A life void of purpose will always leave you unfulfilled. One day, I was reading, and I stumbled across a quote by Mark Twain that said, "The two most important days in your life are the day you are born and the day you find out why." I read that quote and it felt like something punched me in the gut and knocked the wind out of me. In that moment, I realized I had no clue why I was born. I got angry with God, and I began to think over my life and remember every bad thing that ever happened to me. There was nothing I could extrapolate from my past that even resembled anything good or purposeful. I went into a rage asking God why he allowed me to be born to endure the madness I went through? "Why Me? I was just a child. I was innocent, and I did not ask for any of this." I was talking and yelling for what seemed to be hours, complaining about my lot in life. When I was all cried out, in a still small voice, God said, "Your scars have purpose."

Abba spoke to me so gently and said, "I am healing the wounds, but I will not remove the scars because you will show them to others as a road map to find me." In that moment, I was looking for some outside thing to give God that would please him, and I did not realize the thing he wanted was me. He wanted my fears and all my inadequacies, every broken piece of my life that I deemed unattractive was getting ready to be meat for the master's use. The very next day I received a message from someone who wanted me to talk to a family member about a personal issue. When I did, I found out they had been dealing with the pain of childhood sexual abuse. When I listened to her crying and blaming God for the cards she was dealt, I immediately realized my purpose. I was her less than 24 hours ago, and just that quick God had positioned me to be a voice that brought her clarity and prospective. It was not until I embraced my scars that I realized how powerful they were and how beneficial they would be to the lives of many. A few months after that, my podcast: The Heart of The Matter, was launched as a platform where I could tell my story of healing and restoration to men and women all over.

When we began, I asked a question. Why are you here? I want to revisit that again. Are you truly fulfilling your purpose in the earth? Or are you stumbling past the thing that will bring God the ultimate glory because of the pain it caused. For someone, it might be a divorce, and for another it could be a loss. Whatever it may be could be the very tool God uses to position you for purpose. If someone would have told me that my pain would one day prosper me, I would have laughed in their face, but now that is my reality. It was good that I was afflicted because that crushing produced a very specific glory that now has me about my Father's business. For some, your mouth has been silenced for years, but you are about to open it, and your story will unlock the chains of those that hear it. If you survived anything, you have a responsibility to share with others what God has done. In my journey, I discovered my willingness to tell my story has positioned me for greater levels of personal healing and development.

The Cost of Purpose

Purpose will cost you everything, so are you willing to pay the price necessary to fulfill it. The story of the cross is a story of purpose. Jesus knew his purpose and he understood what he had to do to fulfill it. 1 John 3:8 KJV says, "He that committeth sin is of the devil, for the devil sinneth from the beginning. For this purpose, the Son of God was manifested, that he might destroy the works of the devil." In this passage, I want to highlight two things. Before you can Identify your purpose, you must identify the problem you were born to solve. For Jesus, the problem he was born to solve was sin. Sin was a problem that needed to be fixed. What problem plagues you and leaves you with a burning desire to solve it? What frustrates you and keeps you up at night? What consumes your focus and aggravates you when you see it neglected? That might be your purpose. After you have identified the what, you must figure out the how.

After the problem is established, the how can be revealed. In this passage, the remedy for solving the sin problem was destroying the works of darkness. How would Jesus fulfill this task? The answer is with his life. When you are walking in purpose, it will cost you everything. It may not be a literal death like Jesus experienced, but something will have to die. The death may be to your human reasoning or to your fear. To some, it may be to die to the opinions of others and the plans they had for your life. Every assignment that produces glory will require a death. The question is "How bad do you want it?" Jesus knew what it would take for him to fulfill his destiny, and that road was not easy. He had to endure shame, betrayal, and agony to fulfil what he was sent here to do. All throughout scripture, we read how Jesus would boldly say the words, "I came to do the will of the one who sent me." This should be our stance as well, to boldly and unapologetically live a life that is pleasing to the Father, a life so full of purpose and glory that the on looker sees the Father's image in all we do. This sort of purposeful living is going to cost you something, but as a child of God, we are assured that any suffering or agony it causes is not worthy to be compared to the glory God will reveal in us. I would rather suffer in purpose than to die unfulfilled. When I leave this earth, it is my hope to live a life completely poured out.

Everything that I have ever endured; the good, the bad, and the ugly will be a means to give God praise. If it were not for the brokenness, I would have never known him as a healer. If it had not been for the betrayal, I would not have known him as a friend that sticks closer than a brother. If I never experienced a broken heart, I would have never known him to be a mender. Therefore, I have learned to give him thanks in all things because he is sovereign, and he makes no mistakes. In closing, I want to encourage you to embrace your scars. Do not hide them. Reveal them for the glory of God. The revealing of your scars may be the key to making others believe. John 20:25-27 (Good News Translation) states, "So, the other disciples told him. 'We have seen the Lord!' Thomas said to them, 'Unless I See the scars of the nails in his hands and put my fingers on those scars and my hand in his side, I will not believe.' A week later, his disciples were again inside, and Thomas was with them. The doors were locked, but Jesus came and stood among them and said, 'Peace be with you.' Then, he said to Thomas, 'Put your finger here and look at my hands! Put your hand into my side. Stop doubting and have Faith!'"

Thomas was reassured when he saw Jesus's scars. The doubter was now a believer, and his faith had made in whole. How many freedoms are connected to your scars? There could be an entire generation of witnesses waiting on you to reveal the wounds you endured on your journey. Will you boldly unveil them as testimonies of the power of God? Will you turn that which the enemy meant for bad into a tool for good? Can you see the beauty behind the pain and understand the God you serve does not make mistakes? It is only then you will truly understand that you were "Scarred for Purpose."

_____
_____
_____
_____
_____
_____
_____
_____
_____
_____
_____
_____
_____
_____
_____

Her Beauty Isn't Your Beast
By Dae'l Pasco

The childhood of most little girls is full of cartoons, fairytales, and stories about love. From a young age, we are intentionally groomed by someone to embrace love stories that seem unreal and become the perfect woman for a man that we will one day meet. Although I thoroughly enjoyed stories of love, in cartoon form, I was never one to focus on the lovey-dovey parts or even allocate time to imagine one day being the one sharing parts of God's heart with others in such a deep way. I simply enjoyed the music, snark jokes and the crazy situations the characters would end up in as a result of their own desires, lack of self-worth, and how their imagination always kept them in a place of believing for something "fairytailish." Unbeknownst to me, God was always meeting me as I'd watch these movies, and He'd share revelation that always left me mind-blown and in a state of awe.

As a little girl, Beauty and the beast is one of the movies that I loved to watch, and it wasn't until I wrote this piece that God even allowed me to receive such a stupefying revelation. Although I now see that Beauty and the beast is promoting bestiality, which is a discussion for a later time. There is a more sobering message that can be taken into account. No matter which rendition I've watched, they've all kept the storyline in tact...A man becomes a beast and meets a beautiful woman who helps him to un-become so vile.

Beauty and the beast is about a prince who was turned into a beast due to his own inability to love. Love for others wasn't the only issue at hand, even though he struggled with vanity, unappreciation, and a lack of love for himself.

His lack of love gave permission to a "witch" to bind him with a spell that could only be disempowered by an encounter with true love. This spell isolated him, made him unkind, easily agitated, and an outcast. Honestly, I don't believe his poor character was the result of the spell. I believe the spell further revealed what was already in his heart.

It is so amazing how what lies in our hearts are revealed through situations and the actions of other people. Although what they do provoke a response, the truth is... are responses are only a clear indication of what was already in us that aren't so beautiful. Yet and still, there are times we choose to ignore the beast within our deceitful hearts that God tries to reveal, situation-after-situation. Beast was known to live a lonely life in a mansion with household items that kept him company. They'd serve him and were frequently reminded that they served no other purpose but to do so. It's mind-blowing to me that they were once fully functional humans but, became appliances because of their association with the prince. A spell that was intended for one person affected everyone around him simply because of influence, proximity, and relationship. Isn't it crazy how our association with someone introduces either the blessing of God, or a curse - simply because of relationship? We'll dig into this a bit more in a moment.

A while after the spell had been casted and the prince became a beast, an unwelcome visitor frantically knocked on his door. This man was known to be Maurice... the town weirdo and inventor. Days before arriving at the beast's door, Maurice had an encounter with him in the wilderness. After seeing the abnormally huge beast with his own eyes, he ran into town to inform everyone of what he'd just experienced. The people laughed him to scorn and didn't believe what they had heard. As a result, Maurice was locked up and sent away...taken to the beast's home in a carriage, where he was locked up again.

Maurice had a beautiful, unique, and mysterious daughter named Belle. Knowing that was odd for her father to not return home, she went on a quest to find him during the night, only to come into the knowledge that he'd been put away by the people in town. Belle (meaning beauty) decided to search for her father and bring him home. Unknowingly, she ended up at the door of the beast.

She knocked on his door and decided to walk inside to take a look around. During her time of exploration, the beast informed her that Maurice was locked away and would remain in captivity for the rest of his life, but Belle asked that her father be set free in exchange for her life.

Although Belle's request touched the heart of Beast, and he was extremely shocked by this, he decided to allow her father to go free and keep Belle as she had suggested. In conclusion, Belle played a major part in the transformation of Beast's heart. She showed kindness, compassion, and love – even when the beast continued to be stubborn and inconsiderate. Because of her inward and outward makeup, the beast's heart changed, and the spell was broken, simply because love conquered all.

The story of Beauty and the beast is just that...a story made-up for entertainment. However, there is a vital Girl Code that can be found in the storyline. Beast's outward appearance changed to resemble exactly what His heart was full of. Before his outward transformation, the prince was handsome and desired by many. His heart is what pushed people away, leaving him in a space to only dwell on the negativity in his heart and a state of hopelessness because...who would ever give a beast a chance to find love and change? He had a major decision to make. Either he played the victim and blamed others for his current outcome because of his choice to reject love, or he accepted responsibility, open his heart and allow the beauty that knocked on his door a space to show him what love truly was.

How many times have we as women allowed the beauty of another woman to be what we deemed as our personal beast? How many times has God presented an opportunity for us to connect with a woman who exuded beauty, only to sabotage the connection because our past experiences and current hurts were speaking to us about her, louder than we allowed the voice of the Lord to? How many times did you see another woman's beauty as a device that would come to break down the lie that you'd been rehearsing, but because you weren't mature enough to embrace love, you made her a beast to remain in your false state of beauty?

These tricks of the enemy happen so often. Our personal lack of confidence in God, awareness of who we are in Him, ill motives as to why we do what we do, and lack of belief in the vision for our lives has the ability to trap us in this space of envy, jealousy, competition, intimidation, aggravation and hatred. Two stories immediately came to mind as I pondered on this....the story of two sisters, Mary and Martha, and the story of two men, Saul and David. As we look into each of these examples, we'll see how everything mentioned above were the root issues that caused some of these people to become casualties to their own inward vices, pushing away the very beauty that God placed in their lives to help them to destroy the beast within.

Mary and Martha

As they continued their travel, Jesus entered a village. A woman by the name of Martha welcomed him and made him feel quite at home. She had a sister, Mary, who sat before the master, hanging on every word he said. But Martha was pulled away by all she had to do in the kitchen. Later, she stepped in, interrupting them. "Master, don't you care that my sister has abandoned the kitchen to me? Tell her to lend me a hand." The master said, "Martha, dear Martha, you're fussing far too much and getting yourself worked up over nothing. One thing only is essential, and Mary has chosen it—it's the main course, and it won't be taken from her" [Luke 10:38-42 MSG].

Many times, this story is told from a place that what Martha was doing was wrong and unnecessary, but this isn't the case at all. Martha choosing to show Jesus hospitality was very honorable. However, her response shows that she was frustrated and didn't understand the opportunity that was before her, which pushed her into a place of comparison with her sister and open rebuke from Jesus. Mary chose to sit at the feet of Jesus and soak in everything that He was exuding. Her focus was on Him and Him alone. She probably had no issues with helping Martha show hospitality, but her relationship with Him was what mattered most, and she didn't want to miss out on that moment. Who's to say that she wouldn't have assisted moments after, had Martha first come correct, and they all spent some intimate time together. Martha's focus was not even on Jesus. The KJV of this passage says, Martha was cumbered about much service.

Simply put, her servitude was a hinderance, overload, burden and inconvenience.

"Come to Me, all who are weary and heavily burdened [by religious rituals that provide no peace], and I will give you rest [refreshing your souls with salvation]. Take My yoke upon you and learn from Me [following Me as My disciple], for I am gentle and humble in heart, and you will find rest (renewal, blessed quiet) for your souls. For My yoke is easy [to bear] and My burden is light."

When God places it on our hearts to do a thing, it won't feel burdensome. It won't be an inconvenience, and truth be told, we won't even care about those who aren't "in the kitchen" helping us to serve because it's coming from a sincere place. When we hear God, worrying about the next woman isn't our concern because we know and understand God always sends assistance and will find her at the right time. Mary never once pointed out Martha's position because she wasn't focused on Martha. She wanted to get all that she could from her Lord. Martha was a busy body and was working to keep her mind off of her internal issues. How do I know this? Luke 10:41-42 says, "Martha, Martha, thou art careful and trouble about many things, but one thing is needful, and Mary hath chosen that good part, which shall not be taken away from her."

Jesus was there to work on their internal being. Do you know how many "beasts" are tamed and evicted from our inward parts, simply because we choose to sit in the Lord's presence. Do you think it was a coincidence that Martha is always seen as the busy body? When Jesus knocks on our door, we either willfully sit before him and allow Him to expose everything within us and the motives of our heart, or we find reasons to get busy so that what's inside of us isn't revealed, which is the ultimate plan of the enemy. As long as we're "too busy" and occupied, Jesus can't get a word in, our true beauty can't be revealed, and beasts won't be exposed. In this, tension is created, division happens, and aggravation with someone intended to be a sister overrides genuine relationship due to a lack of understanding and stillness.

Martha was working for approval while Mary was resting and being approved. As sisters, why we do what we do matters. If we don't understand what we are to be doing, why we are to do it, and what we should be doing, we'll go to God trying to condemn the very one who is actually living in a place of grace from the revelation of the beauty of Jesus.

Saul and David

So, David went out wherever Saul sent him. He acted wisely and prospered, and Saul appointed him over the men of war. And it pleased all the people and also Saul's servants. "As they were coming [home], when David returned from killing the Philistine, the women came out of all the cities of Israel, singing and dancing, to meet King Saul with tambourines, [songs of] joy, and [a]musical instruments. The women sang as they played and danced, saying, 'Saul has slain his thousands, And David his ten thousands.' Then, Saul became very angry, for this saying [b]displeased him; and he said, "They have ascribed to David ten thousands, but to me they have ascribed [only] thousands. Now what more can he have but the kingdom?' Saul looked at David with suspicion [and jealously] from that day forward" (1 Samuel 18:5-9 AMP). Jealousy is something I've had to face my entire life. I remember encountering that spirit as early as the 1st grade; however, God made it known to me that the sexual abuse that I endured happened as a result of my baby sister's choice to not resolve her own issues, which caused her to be jealous of little girls, abusing them and inviting others in to do the same. Crazy right? A grown woman viewing a toddler as someone to envy and ultimately wanting to damage her because of her own pain. The devil doesn't care who he targets with any of his devices, but jealousy is one that will creep into the heart of anyone who is open and willing to be used by it.

Song of Solomon 8:6 speaks about the jealousy of God how powerful it is and how cruel it will become in order for us to know His love for us. Many times, this scripture, along with others have been twisted to make it seem as though He is jealous of us but, through revelation and knowing who God is, that couldn't be any further from the truth. He is jealous for us, not of us, and trust…there is a major difference between the two. Sadly, this is not the jealousy that we may permeate or receive from others. The jealousy that we experience at the hand of man is indeed cruel, and when not caught in time... leads to hatred.

Per Webster's definition, jealousy is a disposition, attitude, or feeling; it also means to alertly watch, especially to avoid danger. The Passion Translation of Proverbs 14: 30 says, "A tender, tranquil heart will make you healthy, but jealousy can make you sick." The Message version puts it this way, "Sound mind makes for a robust body, but runaway emotions corrode the bones." When jealousy is not addressed and done so quickly, infirmities come onto the one whose heart it full of it.

It amazes me how Saul went from being the one God used when Israel was looking for a king to being the man that was once used by God in such great magnitude. Something stood out to me while reading 1 Samuel 10 that I'd never seen. 1 Samuel 10:27 says, "But the children of Belial said, 'How shall this man save us?' And they despised him and brought him no presents. But he held his peace." Is it possible that because of the lack of honor and affirmation, Saul felt the need to over perform so that he could be accepted by man? Although it was said that Saul was great in stature, he didn't seem to have much confidence, and he often disobeyed what God instructed him to do. Saul's impatience always seemed to lead him to a place of doing just enough. His heart was revealed even the more, each time. As a result of his disobedience to God and his people pleasing ways, the kingdom was taken away from him and given to another man, which you may know to be David, the son of Jesse.

Honestly, the demands that people place on God and man have the ability to play a major part in our exaltation and demise. Israel demanded a king, even though they had the greatest King of all leading them... God. However, because they wanted to be like other nations, and they wanted a king that could fight their battles [1 Samuel 8:20], they demanded the Prophet Samuel seek God and provide them a King. Although God told them of all of the detriments of no longer having Himself as their personal King, they still wanted what they felt was right. This placed man on the throne of their hearts and moved God from his rightful place.

Remember when I said God is jealous for us? Yep! This had a lot to do with what Saul went through. Although God allowed their desires to be met, and He was well aware that they would ask for a king before they did, man was never intended to have dominion over another man. Thankfully God gives us this beautiful thing called grace, but we must be careful with the positions we push man into because that could set him up for failure and great pain.

I believe Saul never intended to have God's spirit taken from him. I believe his motives were absolutely pure when he first set out to do what was instructed of him. However, he may not have been aware of his short comings and how they'd be targeted, whether intentionally or unintentionally by man, which would further reveal his own beasts. When the Spirit of The Lord departed from Saul, an evil spirit from the Lord troubled him. [1 Samuel 16:14] Say what! An evil spirit from the Lord troubled him. Yes, an evil spirit FROM the Lord troubled him, not an evil spirit OF the Lord. God is not evil; He does however have the ability to command a spirit and tell it how to operate. Does this mean, God wanted this to be the outcome? I don't believe so, God always has the best intentions when He creates, appoints, or instructs us to do a thing. "But every man is tempted, when he is drawn away of his own lust, and enticed" [James 1:14].

When you are tempted, don't ever say, "God is tempting me." God is incapable of being tempted by evil, and he is never the source of temptation. Instead, it is each person's own desires and thoughts that drag them into evil and lure them away into darkness. Evil desires give birth to evil actions. And when sin is fully mature it can murder you! So, my friends, don't be fooled by your own desires [James 1:13-16].

When Saul met David, he loved him greatly; and he became his armourbearer [1 Samuel 16:21]. David was also the one who would play the harp for Saul when Saul would get into one of his "moods" as he was being tormented and under the influence of an evil spirit. The love that Saul had for David vanished when jealousy took its place. David loved Saul, showed Saul honor -in and out of sight, behaved wisely, and did whatever he was told by Saul- so much so that Saul promoted David over the men or war. The beauty in

David's heart and his character drew attention, and per 1 Samuel 18:5, he was accepted in the sight of all the people, the very thing that Saul was not.

After David returned home from slaughtering Philistines, women of Israel danced and sang to a song that they created. They sang and sang... "Saul hath slain his thousands, and David his ten thousands." Uh oh! There it goes again... comparison from outside sources. David was seen as accomplishing more than Saul. For a man, that is a big deal, and for Saul that was a blow below the belt. Let's just say that from that moment on Saul was jealous of David and kept a close eye on him. He thought so much of David that he knew the only thing left in his possession was the Kingdom and because Samuel had already given him word that the Kingdom was no longer his, Saul pondered on the thought that David would be the next in line to sit on the throne. Because of this, Saul set out to kill David.

Now, if nothing else has blown your mind, this probably will. Saul became jealous simply because of what other people had to say. David didn't say it, not even his own son Samuel. Shoot, it's wasn't even told to him by God. Saul heard the accolades from the mouths of women, and they struck a nerve. How is it that jealousy can come as a result of another being complimented or celebrated if there isn't already something in the heart that resonates with envy or the need to be affirmed. I wouldn't be surprised if we were to take a deeper look into Saul's childhood, only to find a little boy who was not nurtured or affirmed as much as a child should have been. Saul gives us a clue as to where his family came from, and it definitely was not a lineage of kings. He was a Benjamite, the smallest tribe of Israel, to which his family was the least of all of the families of the Tribe of Benjamin [1 Samuel 9:21]. So, not only was his family the smallest, but he was a part of the smallest tribe. When Samuel spoke with him, even Saul asked in so many words, "You actually want to speak with me?" He didn't deem himself worthy of such a discussion, yet alone a position.

When we don't deal with the issues of our heart, in that place that no one knows us, the devil will make it his business to make sure someone or something touches that weak spot so that we fall and lose all that God had in store for us. Not only will things be taken away, but we will have faults with other women (and men) who have nothing to do with our internal beasts. If Saul would have repented and asked God to search his heart, as David had, who knows how the entire situation could have turned out, but Saul continued to try doing things in his own strength. He no longer saw himself as small [1 Samuel15:17] and that was his biggest issue. He was no longer humble before the Lord.

It becomes a sad moment in time when we don't graduate to a new position but have the position taken from us because of our own insecurities and a lack of obedience. To top it off, we have to see someone else walk out the very assignment that was given to us, only to never be provided a chance to fulfill that assignment again.

David was a man after God's own heart; God said this himself. No matter how many times David got it wrong, he always repented and turned away from the evil he'd done and back to God. David continuously showed God that he was nothing without him and there was no way he'd be able to please him in his own strength. Although he had many enemies, he always spoke about his internal beasts that were being used as a downfall and stumbling blocks between him and God. God deems this as a beautiful thing. God saw David's vulnerability and humility as a sign of honor and faith before him. As a result, He never left David. When God sent Samuel to find Saul's replacement, he already knew exactly who to put in place. David had many brothers of great stature, and he would have been the people's choice, even the family's choice. But the Lord said unto Samuel, "Look not on his countenance, or on the height of his stature; because I have refused him: for the Lord seeth not as man seeth; for man looketh on the outward appearance, but the Lord looketh on the heart" [1 Samuel 16:7]. Although it wasn't mentioned, David's brothers may have felt some type of way about his new promotion, and David may have had some issues in his heart about it, but it never put him in a position of dishonor or self-abandonment from God. He always drew nearer.

As sisters, we must understand that we will come across other women who can do things that we cannot. They may obtain a level of influence that we never do. These women may have an outward and inward beauty that places them in positions that are desirable and celebrated. We'll be connected to women who don't have the insecurities we do and may have never been exposed to the pains we have. These women may have different interests just as Mary and Martha, but that's all ok. Our sisters are not our competition, neither are they our enemies. The only enemy we have is the devil. "Your hand-to-hand combat is not with human beings but with the highest principalities and authorities operating in rebellion under the heavenly realms. For they are a powerful class of demon-gods and evil spirits that hold this dark world in bondage" [Ephesians 6:12 TPT]. Our sisters do not fit this description.

If and when you find yourself in a state of envy, jealousy, competition, intimidation, aggravation and hatred, check your own heart. Yes, there are things that people do that will agitate, but our response and heart's posture is our responsibility. God allows for these things to happen so that we don't act as Saul and turn away from him, but as David…running into His loving arms every time. Jealousy is a result of disbelief and a lack of confidence in who God created you to be. Why be jealous of what others possess, when God has a whole storehouse with your name on it? I'm not even referencing cars, clothes, or anything materialistic but, inward possessions. God has placed beautiful treasures inside of you. He created you with a huge portion of your heart that only you can reveal to the world. There are attributes of God that only you carry, people that only you were designed to impact in the way that you do, and fights that only He can use you to tackle because others wouldn't last. This isn't about comparison but embracing who you are in Him and how He desires to use you to serve Him for His glory.

Things about jealousy to keep in mind: Don't allow others to compare you to another. If/when comparison is made, find something to exemplify in the other individual instead of meditating on what was pointed out as a strength of theirs and weakness of yours, and vice versa.

Know that there is only one you, and God didn't make any copies. Comparison kills authenticity. Live in God's truth, your design, and without apology no matter what it takes. Do not compromise who you are. Jealousy, if not corrected, will always lead to hate and murderous thoughts. Guard your heart and mind by acknowledging ill feelings quickly. If this means you have to tell the other person about these feelings, do so. Hold yourself accountable.

Don't let ill thoughts linger, only to gain more power in your mind. One of the enemy's greatest tactics is the spirit of division. He desires that we as God's daughters be divided because there is great power in unity. We need echoer, but we are of no good when we are against one another or envying what the other has. We do damage to the kingdom of darkness when we are on one accord. You are your sister's keeper. When you don't cover her and you choose to expose her, you are giving the enemy free reign...really only hurting yourself. Your admiration of her beauty and strength can be used as armor against the enemy and his tricks. Remember... Her Beauty is Not Your Beast.

Her beauty is a reflection of your Father and an extension of your body. Her beauty may be used to tame and eradicate the beasts that lie in your heart, only if you allow her beauty to shine. Shutting her down doesn't help her or you in any way, shape or form. Your beauty does the same to her beasts. The beautiful thing about this is that the beasts inside of us are truly God's responsibility. It's just that at times, we need assistance to identify them and remove them, who better than a sister who is equipped to help you?

Questions to ponder:

1. What does jealousy mean to me?
2. Is there anyone in my life that I am jealous of? If yes, why?
3. Is there anyone who is jealous of me? How can I help their mind to be loosed from the spirit of jealousy and hate? Did I play a part in their disdain toward me?
4. If you find that you are constantly targeted by jealousy, how does this make you feel, and what do you plan to do in order to combat what's being projected towards you?
5. How will you make sure to see her beauty as a gift and not something that over shines who you are?
6. How does God use your beauty to destroy the works of beast in the lives of your sisters?

I Promise...
-Love always, God,
The Promise Keeper

By: Dacia Carter

"Way maker..." I began to sing the lyrics to that song with a shattered heart in May of 2020. In that very moment, I was desperately trying to convince myself that God was in fact the promise keeper I was singing about. In the blink of an eye, God came to test every single word I declared about him. He came to test every single dance of intercession I danced concerning his kingdom and my destiny. Everything, and I mean everything, was up for grabs for the enemy to come and snatch because I was weak and didn't have any strength in me to fight. So, I thought, "Is he really a promise keeper? Look what he did to you! He lied to you twice. Two failed engagements. He doesn't love you. He will never fulfill the promise of marriage for you. THAT promise doesn't apply to you. You're such a dummy. Your life is a mess, what do you have to show for all your sacrifices? God is never going to fulfill his promises concerning you." Those were all the thoughts that begin to speak louder and echo in my mind.

Many times, when we get hurt and experience heartbreak, we say we are numb to pain, but I beg to differ because when one is numb to something there is absolutely no feeling. Being numb wasn't my case. In fact, the pain and agony I was feeling was almost unbearable. This pain my heart was experiencing was literally driving me to insanity. It was as if my memory had been wiped cleaned of everything I knew about God. Have you ever been to the place where you couldn't think of one, just one scripture to quote? This is the place I was at. Heartbreak can sometimes cause you to question your entire existence. This is exactly what was happening to me. Was I going to allow this heartbreak to build my faith, or was I going to fold?

"Journey to the Promise Land" was a captivating and cute theme for my wedding. However, the journey isn't so pretty. You see, the majority of the time God will show us the end of the journey. The ending that's revealed to us is always encouraging, beautiful, motivating, exciting, and gives us just enough faith we need to get started. However, the entire purpose of the journey is to beautifully break and transform us to look more like Christ. Let's take a look at Abraham and Sarah. God makes a promise to Abraham. Genesis 12:1-3 says, "Get out of your country, from your family and from your father's house, to a land that I will show you. I will make you a great nation; I will bless you and make your name great; And you shall be a blessing. I will bless those who bless you, And I will curse him who curses you; And in you all the families of the earth shall be blessed." God came and obliterated Abraham's comfort zone. Not only did God come for his comfort zone, He immediately challenged his faith. Everything about the instructions he was given was risky. Everything about faith is risky. Nothing about having faith is safe. When God makes you a promise, he is going to break all your little rules, precepts, thoughts, plans, agendas, and so much more. God revealed the end of the journey to him. God left out the part of it being a twenty-five-year journey for him and Sarah to obtain the promise. Did you know that after God makes a promise to you, he is going to send a contradiction? LOL, ironic, right? As soon as Abraham followed God's instructions, he was led to a place that totally contradicted what God spoke to him. This land in Egypt was in a famine. Also, Abraham feared he would be killed, and the Egyptians would take his wife. I think we underestimate the power of fear and the destruction it can cause in our lives if it goes unchecked and not dealt with. Fear spoke so loud to Abraham that he forgot just that fast what God promised him. God said he was going to bless him and make his name great. Therefore, there was no way the Egyptians could have killed him or Sarah because he had unfulfilled promises that hadn't been manifested yet. You see, when God makes a promise, that means it's a legally binding declaration that gives the person to whom it is made a right to expect or to claim the performance or forbearance of a specified act. When God makes a promise, it is sealed in heaven and cannot be broken. God is very intentional with the words he speaks. He doesn't talk just to talk. The Bible tells us in Numbers 23:19, "God is not a man that he should lie, nor is he the son of man that he should repent. Hath he said it and shall he not do it? Or has he spoken it and shall he not make it good?" Let's pause for a second.....

Activity #1:

I want you to take a moment and reflect on the promises God has made to you. Have they been fulfilled? Have you allowed fear to punk you out of continuing the journey? Where in the journey did you stop believing God, and why? After this reflection, write out a faith confession. In this faith confession, you will rededicate yourself to the journey. Look up five scriptures of faith and speak them over your journey. Remind God of what he promised you. Keep the faith confession in a place you have access to, so you will be able to confess your faith to God often.

Trusting God and having faith can sometimes be one of the toughest things we have to do. Sometimes all we have is the word from the Lord. Having faith is going to trigger several emotions such as frustration, anger, uncertainty, anxiety, fear, doubt, and unbelief. However, God deals with each emotion and help brings us to a healthy resolve internally. When God makes us a promise, he is after our wholeness. Sometimes we do not recognize our brokenness in certain areas until we are tested in our faith. For instance, Zacharias didn't know he was broken until God came to test his faith. In Luke 1, The angel of the Lord came to deliver a message from God, stating he and his wife Elisabeth would bare a son, and his name would be John. By the time this message was delivered to Zacharias, his heart had already been shattered from the disappointments and past failures of life. Instead of believing God and taking him at his word, Zacharias representatives of his memory begin to speak for him. What do I mean by that? He immediately remembered all of the times he and his wife believed for a child and came up empty handed. Time and time again. Why? Because he responded in doubt (Luke 1:18). Did you know it is an insult to God and his character when we doubt him? The Bible tells us its faith that pleases God. That means, we can be successful, fulfill our dreams, save souls, serve others, and God would not be pleased with us. Many times, we pray, "God I want to live a life pleasing unto you." If we live a life of faith, it is guaranteed God would be pleased with us. Abraham, Sarah, and Zacharias eventually yielded to the process of God. Their journey was tough. They experienced so many trials, tribulations, frustrations, and disappointments along the way, but God kept his promise! I want to encourage you that no matter what it looks like God is a promise keeper. He doesn't withhold good things from us. I encourage you to stay on the journey to your promise land. Don't give up. I wanted to give up on my journey, but I chose to level up in my faith and not fold. I now sing the song "Way Maker" from the mountaintops.

Activity #2:
Get an empty wine bottle, place it inside of 5 to 6 plastic grocery bags. Throw it up in the air and allow it to hit the ground to break. Go to a river, pier, or lake. Grab a piece of the glass and confess your disappointments, heart breaks, and anything that hurt you to cause you to doubt God. You can go back as far as your childhood. Confess anything that hurt. Then throw the piece of glass into the water (sea of forgetfulness). Get another piece of glass and do the same things until all the pieces are in the water. Once you are done, the next time God makes you a promise, or challenges you to make a faith move, the representative of faith will speak and respond to God instead of the memories of your past hurts and failures.

Remember, God is a promise keeper, and he is going to fulfill every single promise he has promised you.

Meet the Authors

Authoress **Brittney B. Hoover**
FB: Bee Loved
YouTube: Brittney Hoover
IG: unadulterated_truth

Brittney B. Hoover is a woman of many gifts and positions. She is not only a lover of Jesus Christ but also a wife to an amazing husband, Michael Hoover, a daughter to a powerful, kingdom couple- Pastor Kelvin and Glenda Broadwater, friend, sister, educator, and a host of other divine callings. She is a resident of McComb, MS by way of Jackson, MS and finds joy in writing, speaking and operating in her spiritual gift of encouraging others. Brittney has published "It is Finished: A Devotional of Unadulterated Truth" and co-authored "Victory Over It All 22 Days of Healing, Deliverance and More" with her husband. Currently, Brittney enjoys pouring into others, specifically women and children and looks forward to many more opportunities to do so. Brittney believes God to be a healer, deliverer and waymaker! Having experienced depression, suicidal thoughts and attempts, relationship and financial hardships, etc., she is able to relate to others who experience the same. Truly, our experiences shape and mold us into more equipped and capable sounding boards for Jesus Christ. It is in the depth of our valleys that God operates most profoundly. Without him, we are nothing and can do nothing. Brittney says, "As long as God is pleased, everything will always work out for our good. It is his promise, and God is not a man that he should lie. That's the living word."

> "God sees ME. It sounds so simple, yet it is one of the most profound revelations I ever came to know. Despite what it looks like, God sees me, and he is forever with me. He's forever with you as well. God sees you, believe that."
>
> **- Brittney Hoover**

Authoress **Tiffany Lindsey**
IG & YouTube: Tiffanyishername
Website: Readingwithtiffany.com

Tiffany is a wife and mother from Houston, Texas. She has a passion for literacy and children and has been working in the field of education for a decade. Along with that, Tiffany has also served in the children's ministry at church. Her purpose is to help children any way she can, whether it be inside of a school building or outside.

"If I had things my way, I would merely be doing good things, but because of obedience I'm doing God things"

- **Tiffany Lindsey**

Authoress **Jasmine Joseph**
Instagram: @Jasmineajoseph
YouTube: Jasmine A. Joseph
Twitter: Jasmineajoseph
Website: www.Jasmineajoseph.com

Jasmine Joseph is the epitome of a woman on a mission. After spending her teenage years seeking fulfillment from the world, at the age of 21 she had an encounter with Jesus that changed her life forever. Not only is Jasmine a business major, she is also a blogger, youtuber, and business owner. As the founder and visionary of "My Budget Binder," Jasmine is on a mission to educate current and future generations to steward well while eradicating poverty and financial illiteracy. She is an advocate for Jesus, the gospel, stewardship, business, authenticity and being fine while doing it all. Jasmine fearlessly encourages women that they can love Jesus, be dope, and confident.

"Your intersection for faith, beauty, and business"

- Jasmine Joseph

Authoress **MoNique Perkins**

Monique Perkins is a native of Tampa, FL and the Proud Mother of two amazing children. (Iyanna and Clarence Jr.) Monique is a Partner of The Center for Manifestation under the leadership of Apostle Mark T. Jones. Monique's ministry began in the area of the Arts, where she traveled and taught Dance for over 15 years. Monique's ministry assignment shifted in the last several years after she truly allowed God to deal with her areas of brokenness. She is the founder of The Heart of the Matter, a blog and podcast that focuses on dealing with issues of the heart that keep us from relating in a healthy way. Monique is a firm believer that once the heart is healed then the rest of the body must align to it. Monique is also an author and is currently studying to be a public speaker. It is her passion to take the Kingdom message into the secular arena, and not just limit it to the four walls of the church.

"Without my scars I would have no purpose. Without pain, my pursuit would be in vain. I've embraced my scars and I display them unapologetically...Without them there would be no me."

- Mo'Nique Perkins

Authoress **Teairra Barnes**
Instagram: Gemswithtea

Teairra is a millennial woman born in D.C. and raised in Prince George's County, Maryland. She is a mother who has been blessed with three wonderful children. Teairra is someone with a heart for the people. One major assignment she knows she's been called in the world to do is to help whoever she comes in contact with to receive and accept the love of God. She's an active community advocate in her area. Teairra has a passion for children, women, and helping others who are experiencing domestic violence. Her vision consists of being able to let love conquer the world.

"Love will conquer. It can't fail you!"

- Teairra Barnes

Authoress **Dae'l Pasco**
YouTube: Dae'l Pasco
Website: www.Daelkpasco.com

Dae'l Pasco is a faith and fashion blogger who loves simplifying the complexities of life. Dae'l is dedicated to hyping women up to living their most authentic lives, unapologetically and on purpose. She is the wife of Darrell Pasco and mother of Zariiah. When Dae'l isn't writing or creating, you can find her near a body of water, relaxing and thinking of master plans.

"There's nothing mediocre about you. Do things big because that's how God created you to live"

- Dae'l Pasco

Authoress **Dacia Munn**
(formerly Carter, as the book went to print Dacia got married!)
Instagram/YouTube: God the promise keeper
Facebook: God, The Promise Keeper

Dacia Munn, a native of Tampa, FL is a happily married wife, mother of a beautiful daughter, and a full-time student at Full Sail University. Dacia continues to explore and influence the arts. In September 2015, she graduated from L.I.F.T (Ladies Influencing their Future Today) under the mentorship of Layesha Walton. Her mission has fully taken off since then. She has choreographed several productions for the Revolution Fine Arts Ministry and Studio 28, is the director of Freedom in His Movement at the Center for Manifestations, and is the Tampa director for 13:46 Dance Ensemble. In addition to those things, she has successfully produced three theatrical productions for 13:46 Dance Ensemble and hosted her sixth conference with The Annual Life Prophetic Arts Movement in Spring 2021. Nonetheless, this is all just the beginning of a profound work that God is doing through her. And, just as her favorite scripture says, God certainly has great plans for her beyond this (Jeremiah 29:11). Ultimately her mission is to advance the Kingdom of God and reconcile others back to Christ through the arts.

" If God said it, that settles it! #Periodt"

- Dacia Munn

Visionary, Authoress **Ashley Porter**
Instagram: Ashley_Speaks_
Facebook: Girl Code Collective
Website: www.GirlCodeCollective.com

There's no escaping the calling on your life. No one knows that better than Ashley A. Porter affectionately known as Ashley Speaks-The Purpose Visionary, who not only embraces her divine purpose but helps others do the same. Through published books, empowerment speaking/ teaching, and personal development/purpose coaching.

Ashley is committed to destroying generational curses and reclaiming family unity. Building a family legacy is imperative to Ashley.

Ashley is a certified life coach and has earned a Bachelor's degree in Biblical Studies. She is currently pursuing a master's degree in leadership and a doctorate degree in counseling. As the founder of Girl Code Collective, Ashley partners with women through coaching, teaching, and mentorship. Girl Code Collective is a place where women thrive unapologetically.

Ashley enjoys traveling, loving, and laughing with her son, and effectively helping others thrive in their purpose. She's a multi-talented soul with many skills.

" If you have a pulse, you have a purpose"

- **Ashley A. Porter**

www.ingramcontent.com/pod-product-compliance
Lightning Source LLC
Chambersburg PA
CBHW050654160426
43194CB00010B/1935